Ancient
Trees

Kew

ROYAL BOTANIC GARDENS

Ancient Trees

Trees that live for a thousand years

**Edward Parker &
Anna Lewington**

BATSFORD

First published in the
United Kingdom in 2012 by
Batsford, 10 Southcombe
Street, London W14 0RA

An imprint of Anova Books
Company Ltd

ISBN: 978 1 84994 058 0

A CIP catalogue record for
this book is available from
the British Library.

19 18 17 16 15 14 13 12
10 9 8 7 6 5 4 3 2 1

Reproduction by Rival
Colour Ltd, UK
Printed and bound by 1010
Printing International,
China

Contents

Foreword

I am fortunate in having a wonderful job as the head of the arboretum at the Royal Botanic Gardens, Kew, and to have travelled extensively across the globe with my work, observing and collecting seeds and herbarium specimens of trees to maintain and improve the scientific value of the temperate woody plant collections in the arboretum.

One of my first seed-collecting expeditions was in 1985, to the temperate regions of Chile, where there are some incredible forests and amazing trees, including some very rare ones that in cultivation can only be found in specialist collections. It was here that I saw my first exceptionally large ancient trees of around 2,000 years old in their native habitat, the Cordillera de Nahuelbuta in the Araucanía region of Chile. These trees were monkey puzzles (*Araucaria araucana*). As we rounded the bend of a dirt track on our way to the mountains, we came upon a breathtaking sight: the distant horizon, with the architectural silhouettes of this uniquely shaped tree dominating the skyline, gave me a memory that will be with me for the rest of my life. Even though I was familiar with this tree, common in gardens at home, I was nonetheless fascinated by this pure forest of prehistoric-looking living fossils, and I needed to know and understand more about the natural history and ecology of this incredible relic.

We spent several days botanizing and collecting, among some of the largest monkey puzzles that I have ever seen and am ever likely to see again, their bases resembling giant elephant's feet and their distinctive, dark-barked trunks rising up into the foggy skies, where their branched tops dominate. Later into the six-week expedition we ventured further south in Chile to see the alerces (*Fitzroya cupressoides*) of Alerce Andino National Park in the Los Lagos region of the Andes. Like the monkey puzzle, this is a very rare tree in the wild, threatened with over-exploitation because its highly durable timber is in demand for roof shingles, and to see any specimens of this tree would be a treat. On seeing these magnificent 3,000-year-old monoliths of the Chilean forests, I was even more bewildered and lost for words. They are huge trees, growing to heights of 60m (197ft), with incredibly large boles in comparison with the smaller, cultivated specimens I had seen growing in gardens on the west coast of Scotland, where the climate from the Gulf Stream provides good conditions for growth. While we photographed and studied one extremely large tree, there was an eerie silence except for the roar of the river and a few birds, and every time I pass the 4m (13ft) tall specimen by the Redwood Grove at Kew, I am immediately reminded of this moment and transported back to the forest in Chile, clearly picturing these denizens of the forests of Alerce Andino and longing to return one day to catch up with them.

From those two pivotal moments on I became more intrigued by old, historic trees and the stories they hold, increasing my passion for working with trees even further. I love to hear other people's tales of meeting ancient trees, and wherever I am fortunate enough to go botanizing or collecting, I always ask local people if they know of any old or large trees, and relish the opportunity to observe them.

In 2001, while I was travelling in Sichuan, China, our guides, knowing my interest in old trees, took a detour into a village nestling on the banks of the Dadu River called Lengji to see an old maidenhair (*Ginkgo biloba*) tree. As we pulled off the road, the sheer size of this tree was evident, towering above the houses in the village. As we worked our way through the tiny network of paths, we finally reached our target. You can never prepare yourself for what you are about to see, and these first sightings all provide the same exhilarating feeling. The size, the girth and the spread all filled me with awe, but in addition, this tree had a beautiful red temple constructed in its base, complete with incense and candles. This very tree was seen and photographed by our most noted plant collector, Ernest Wilson, in 1908. The entire town came out to see us and were so excited that we had come all the way from England to see their tree that they gave us seeds, which now reside as trees in the arboretum at Kew, a living memory of the 'Lengji Ginkgo'.

I remember my first visit to see the giant redwoods (*Sequoiadendron giganteum*) in Mariposa Grove, Yosemite National Park, in great detail – I had read so much about these revered giants and seen pictures, but nothing could have prepared me for that day. When I first saw 'Grizzly Giant', the largest tree in the park with a diameter of 8.23m (27ft) at its base and over 2,500 years old, it was awe-inspiring: it is an amazing tree, holding itself magnificently far above the surrounding canopy and all the other conifers. This was another special moment in my life, and again I will never be able to describe how I felt; a time to contemplate. That very experience now draws me whenever I can to the west coast of the USA and Canada to witness the giants of the Pacific North-west coast: the coastal redwoods (*Sequoia sempervirens*), the Douglas firs (*Pseudotsuga menziesii*) and the sitka spruces (*Picea sitchensis*).

There is nothing more rewarding and inspiring than seeing these trees residing in their natural habitat, characterful trees that carry so many personal memories or have so many meanings and ethno-botanical links to mankind. It is not always possible for everyone to travel to these remote locations and see them in real life, but we are very lucky that the co-author of this book, Edward Parker, has captured so many of these hugely photogenic, ancient specimens in his photographs, and given everyone the opportunity to meet them. When I need some inspiration and I'm unable to sit under a monkey puzzle in the Araucanía region of Chile, I will sit in the comfort of my home, leafing my way through this wonderful book and being taken back in memory to see some of the ancient trees of the world.

Tony Kirkham
Head of the Arboretum, Royal Botanic Gardens, Kew

INTRODUCTION

The research for this book has taken us on a journey of discovery, not just around the world, but also through time. We have encountered giants whose enormous fluted trunks rise up like great cathedrals, and we have stood in groves of gnarled and wizened trees that were alive before the great pyramids of Ancient Egypt were built, standing in a desolate landscape that has remained virtually unchanged for 20,000 years. We have sensed the quiet power of some of the world's largest and oldest living organisms, and begun to understand the awe and reverence that many peoples in the past have felt. Standing in the presence of some of the world's oldest statesmen, it was impossible not to feel moved and to reflect upon the transience of our own human lives; impossible not to feel that we are part of natural cycles that are just too large for us to comprehend.

At the very beginning of this project, more than ten years ago, we were hoping to include some 24 species of trees that live to over 1,000 years old. As our research progressed, however, we discovered more and more examples of ancient trees from all around the world. The number of candidates has now risen to more than 100 species and the list is still growing. We were intrigued to find that ancient trees occur on all the continents of the globe, with the exception of Antarctica, and that many are easily accessible to millions of people – rural and urban alike. There are 1,000-year-old trees in the Chinese capital, Beijing; within a four-hour drive of Los Angeles; on the outskirts of London; and even close to the largest city in the Amazon rainforest, Manaus. It is pleasing to know that far from being the preserve of explorers and specialists, 1,000-year-old trees are widely enough scattered for many of us to enjoy and visit them easily.

The longevity of trees

No one knows which living tree is currently the oldest in the world or how many tree species produce individuals that live for over 1,000 years. However, we do know the trees with the oldest verifiable ages and almost all are conifers of one sort or another. The oldest living tree today with a full sequence of annual growth rings is a bristlecone pine that stands high in the White Mountains of California and, at the time of writing, is over 4,600 years old. Another bristlecone was believed to have lived for more than 5,000 years. It had 4,862 identifiable rings and a hollow in the middle. Unfortunately these discoveries were made as a result of studying the stump of the tree, which was felled in 1964. Several other trees have been verified to be over 2,000 years old. These include several giant sequoias (*Sequoiadendron giganteum*), which are over 3,000 years old, two

Among all the varied productions with which Nature has adorned the surface of the Earth, none awakens our sympathies, or interests our imagination so powerfully as those venerable trees which seem to have stood the lapse of ages, silent witnesses of the successive generations of man, to whose destiny they bear so touching a resemblance, alike in their budding, their prime and their decay.

JOHN MUIR, 1868

Ancient olive trees growing on Crete. The Minoans introduced olives to this Greek island over 5,000 years ago.

alerce trees (*Fitzroya cupressoides*), also giant conifers that occur in the temperate forests of south-central Chile, one of which has a verifiable age of 3,622 years, the other a recently discovered stump of a felled tree with all 4,080 tree rings intact, and surprisingly, a fig tree. Figs are usually very difficult to age accurately, but the bo tree or bodhi tree (*Ficus religiosa*) at Anuradhapura on the island of Sri Lanka – a cutting from the bodhi tree under which Buddha was said to have gained enlightenment – was planted in a temple garden in 288 BC and has been carefully tended ever since.

The problem with identifying the world's oldest trees is that, apart from counting the entire ring sequence, there is no single foolproof way of calculating the age of many of the most ancient individuals. The most common methods are counting annual tree rings and radiocarbon-dating material taken from the oldest part of the tree. However, both these methods only work on trees that have not become hollow, and involve damaging the tree to some extent in order to take a sample of material for analysis. This means that only a very small proportion of the world's ancient trees can be aged accurately, and that there may be trees even older than the ones listed above.

An estimate of a tree's age can be made from studying the growth rates of trees with known planting dates. For example, a number of ancient yews in the UK have been repeatedly measured, some over hundreds of years, to try and estimate age in relation to the girth of the trunk. In the UK, the Ancient Yew Group (AYG) has recently carried out research which suggests that a yew tree of 7m (23ft) or more in girth should be regarded as ancient and is at least 800 years old. However, it is known that ancient trees grow variably and extremely slowly in old age, leaving experts to speculate on the possible age of trees such as the Fortingall Yew

A thousand-year-old ginkgo tree growing near Seoul in South Korea.

in Scotland, whose hollow trunk was recorded with a circumference of over 16m (52ft) in 1769 by the Honourable Daines Barrington. This could make it 2,000 (or possibly 5,000) years old today.

In the case of most tropical trees, another problem is the absence of growth rings: because of the constant climatic conditions throughout the year, these are never formed. In the absence of hard evidence, it is possible to speculate wildly on the ages of some individuals. The French botanist Michel Adanson (1727–1806), who gave his name to the mighty baobabs (*Adansonia* spp.), caused a sensation in the eighteenth century when he estimated that a giant African tree was 6,000 years old, leading some to question the date of the biblical flood. Recent research on baobab trees in South Africa, however, has indicated that his calculations may not have been too far awry.

Ancient trees are now being discovered with regularity, but the discovery of the first Wollemi pine (*Wollemia nobilis*) in a deep gorge near Sydney in 1994 caused particular excitement, since this represented not just another ancient tree but a whole new species. Wollemi pines closely resemble the fossils of an extinct genus of the Araucariacae family that may date back at least 100 million years. According to Carrick Chambers, who was then Director of Sydney's Royal Botanic Gardens, the discovery was like 'finding a small dinosaur still alive on Earth'. Because of its ability to clone itself by coppicing (the creation of multiple trunks), the Wollemi pine could turn out to be one of the longest-lived species on the planet. The tree known affectionately as the Bill Tree – one of fewer than 100 individuals known to exist – may be more than 1,000 years old. Due to the pine's habit of producing a series of trunks, however, the current trunk of the Bill Tree may in fact be only a few hundred years old, while its rootstock could have been in existence since the time of the Roman Empire.

All around the world, exciting new research on ancient trees is being undertaken. China, for example, is home to a number of ancient ginkgo trees, some of which are considered to be over 3,000 years old; systematic studies are now not only throwing up new 1,000-year-old trees, but revealing the sheer numbers of ancient trees in various parts of the country. Researchers have identified more than 3,800 trees that are over 300 years old in Beijing alone, making it the city with the largest number of ancient trees in the world.

The Chinese modern master painter Xu Beihong wrote in one of his works: 'Beijing is a capital city with the largest number of ancient trees in the world. There are especially numerous cypresses with twisted roots and gnarled branches planted from the Liao (916–1125), Jin (1115–1234), Yuan (1271–1368), and Ming (1368–1644) dynasties. They have gone through the vicissitudes of the ages and are still growing luxuriantly, forming a unique feature of the capital city.'

Other research emerging from tropical countries, such as Vietnam, has extended our understanding of ancient trees in the tropical rainforest, where only two decades ago it was believed that there would be little chance of finding any ancient trees at all. It has been discovered that seasonal monsoon rains cause the laying down of identifiable growth rings in a number of tropical tree species in South East Asia. Tree ring samples taken from *Fokienia hodginsii* trees in Bidoup-Nui Ba National Park near Da Lat, Vietnam, to help with climate studies at Columbia University's Lamont-Doherty Earth Observatory (LDEO) Tree Ring Laboratory, have been discovered to stretch as far back as the year 1029. There may be thousands of ancient trees waiting to be discovered in the rainforests of the world.

What we can say with certainty is that the world's most ancient trees occur in a wide variety of environments around the world, from the temperate climates of Britain and New Zealand to the intense tropical heat of the Amazon rainforest. For some tree species, such as the bristlecone pine, harsh environmental conditions (such as intense cold, high altitude and drought) actually seem to encourage the attainment of great age.

We have also observed that trees can reach ages of over 1,000 years in a variety of ways. In some instances this appears to be related to local environmental conditions; in others it is, fascinatingly, due directly to the intervention of humans. Trees in this category include the olive (*Olea europaea*), sweet chestnut (*Castanea sativa*), oaks (*Quercus* spp.) and limes (*Tilia* spp.), which have regularly been coppiced or pollarded over long periods of time.

For many tree experts and conservationists it is not the actual age of a tree that is of interest, but the process of becoming ancient. The features generally associated with a tree being ancient (for example in an oak or a chestnut) include a wide and hollowing trunk, the presence of epiphytes such as fungi, mosses and lichens, and a lessening of the canopy with dead wood within it, as well as dead wood on the ground. Contrary to widely held belief, these features are not a sign that the tree is about to die, and trees in this condition can remain alive and healthy for many decades, even centuries. These characteristics are all synonymous with being ancient, but because trees grow in a wide variety of environments, they can arrive at this stage at widely differing ages. The more ancient features a tree displays, the more valuable it becomes. This is because the hollows, dead wood and increasing numbers of epiphytes provide habitats for wildlife – some of it very rare. Even after its death, an ancient tree continues to provide habitats for wildlife for decades more. Ted Green, of the Ancient Tree Forum, often points out a dead tree and says 'How can that be a dead tree? It's still full of life.'

Fascinating though this debate is, this book is not designed to identify the world's oldest individual tree or to be a definitive guide to all the world's ancient trees. Rather, it is a celebration of certain tree species and groups of trees containing individuals that are at least 1,000 years old.

Objects of respect

Since the earliest times, trees have held a special fascination for humankind. Across large areas of the world where now only scattered remnants remain, vast forests once stretched unbroken. These forests, the original wildwoods, provided our ancestors with shelter and food, medicines and other necessities, but many of the trees also represented something more. It is not difficult to imagine how, with their huge trunks reaching upwards from the earth and their branches seeming to touch the sky, some of the world's giant and most ancient trees – whose lifespans far exceeded those of human beings – must have seemed immortal and come to occupy a special place within the greater scheme of things; to appear connected with the forces governing the Earth, and to be able to directly influence peoples' lives.

Around the world, many large and slow-growing individual trees have been – and still are for many people today – the objects of deep respect and often a religious reverence, making them sacred and setting them apart from other trees. Such feelings appear to have distinguished one of the most long-living (if not indeed the longest living) of Europe's tree species, the common yew, in the distant past. This tree's mysterious ability to continue to renew itself from a state of apparent decay, and its deadly poisonous but evergreen leaves, helped to confer upon it the status of immortality and place it at the centre of a sacred cult associated with the afterlife. The most common signs of this remain in evidence today in the wealth of ancient yews that still create a deeply mystical aura in churchyards throughout northern Europe.

The great European oaks (*Quercus robur* and *Q. petraea*) and the limes (chiefly *Tilia cordata* and *T. platyphyllos*) also came to acquire a sacred status of their

own – the oaks being associated with the Norse and Germanic gods of thunder and lightning, and the limes with fertility. Sacrifices were made to the powerful supernatural beings associated with these trees, in the hope of influencing the lives of people on Earth. The Celts are a well-known example of a European people whose lives were dominated by trees and the forces they were believed to represent. Describing their tendency to create sacred groves or sanctuaries in forest clearings or glades, the Roman historian Gaius Cornelius Tacitus (AD *c*.55–120) wrote of the Celts living beyond the Roman Empire:

'They deem it incompatible with the majesty of the heavenly host to confine the gods within walls, or to mould them into any likeness of the human face; they consecrate groves and coppices, and they give the divine names to that mysterious something which is visible only to the eyes of faith.'

Such beliefs in the sacred powers or mystical forces of trees are still strongly present in many urban societies today, and are only superficially hidden from view. The familiar Western good-luck charm of 'touching wood' is, for example, according to Jacqueline Memory Paterson, the author of Tree Wisdom, 'a direct continuation of the actions of our Celtic ancestors, who at times of need went to certain trees and touched and communed with them. These trees were thought to contain or house specific spirits, such as those associated with the elements and gods and goddesses.' To many of the world's ethnic groups today which have been able to maintain their cultural traditions (at least in part), trees continue to provide both a practical and a spiritual focus for their lives. One such example is that of the Pehuenche Indians of south-central Chile, whose name and identity have been determined by the monkey puzzle trees (*Araucaria araucana*) among which they have traditionally lived. '*Pehuenche*' means 'people of the monkey puzzle tree', for the tree is sacred to them, and the diet of some communities is still based upon the nutritious seeds produced by the trees. The trees are able to live for an estimated 2,000 years, and once covered a much larger area of the southern

ABOVE LEFT
The bristlecone pine is the world's oldest verifiable tree. One individual has more than 4,600 annual tree rings.

ABOVE CENTRE
Research from the tropics has indicated that rainforest trees may live for much longer than previously thought, with thousand-year-old trees being found in the Amazon region and south-east Asia.

ABOVE RIGHT
Ancient trees, such as this yew in Wales, have been venerated by people all over the world for millennia.

hemisphere. The Pehuenche have been battling for years to save their ancestral forests from international logging concerns, but with only limited success.

On the North American continent, the continued commercial felling of Douglas firs (*Pseudotsuga menziesii*) – some of which were taller than the coast redwoods (*Sequoia sempervirens*) and possibly older than the giant redwoods (*Sequoiadendron giganteum*) – has been the cause of much public concern. This is also true of the continued felling of the coast redwoods, although now only 18 per cent of the remaining forest area falls outside some sort of protection. In the tropics it is now understood that there are almost certainly trees over 1,000 years old that are yet to be discovered, but many of these will disappear because of deforestation. In Europe, the cessation of traditional management systems such as pollarding and coppicing may lead to the early demise of many great trees. In addition, problems now being caused by global warming, in particular drought as well as diseases and pests, threaten forests and trees across the globe.

However, the traditional reverence that has characterized the relationship of entire peoples with certain trees continues to offer these trees some protection. In India, for example, the banyan fig (*Ficus benghalensis*) is protected not only because it has long been considered a sacred tree, but because its shade is greatly valued. Strict regulations control the usage or treatment of banyans for religious and practical reasons; some trees, situated along routes regularly traversed by people on elephants, are reserved for fodder. Similar beliefs are held about the bo tree (*Ficus religiosa*), the sacred fig of India, Sri Lanka and parts of South East Asia, and about the remarkable ginkgo (*Ginkgo biloba*) in China and Korea, which, although almost extinct in the wild, continues to thrive in temple gardens, where it was traditionally planted by Buddhist and other monks.

The remarkable secular uses to which people around the world have put their age-old trees are well illustrated by the baobab and boab trees of Africa and Australia. Here, the hollow trunks of ancient trees have been variously used as prisons, storerooms, lavatories and even pubs. Despite such usage and the fact it cannot be beneficial to their longevity, the trees have been able to survive.

Literary and artistic inspiration

Ancient trees have been a constant source of inspiration to poets, artists and storytellers throughout the ages. William Wordsworth (1770–1850) drew inspiration from ancient yew trees in 'The Pride of Lorton Vale' and refers to the 'fraternal Four of Borrowdale'. For Vincent Van Gogh (1853–90), the subtleties of colour and texture of the olive trees of Provence inspired and drove him to distraction in almost equal measure. Thomas Jefferson (1743–1826) was inspired to write: 'The olive tree is surely the richest gift from heaven', while Aldous Huxley (1894–1963) recorded his feelings as follows: 'I like them all, but especially the olive. For what it symbolizes, first of all – peace with its leaves and joy with its golden oil.' And William Blake's passion for trees was summed up in one of his works, published in 1799, which read:

'The tree that moves some to tears of joy is in the eyes of others only a green thing that stands in the way. Some see Nature all Ridicule and Deformity … and some scarce see Nature at all. But to the eyes of the Man of Imagination, Nature is Imagination itself.'

Ancient trees are precious. There is little else on Earth that plays host to such a rich community of life within a single organism.

SIR DAVID ATTENBOROUGH

Saving our ancient living heritage

Whatever the experts may decide about the exact ages of our oldest trees, a resurgence of interest in saving and appreciating our ancient living heritage has become apparent among people from all walks of life. Ordinary people all over the world, from Chile to Bhutan, are now fighting to save their forests. On an international level, organizations such as **WWF** are continuing to campaign to protect and better manage our forests worldwide by addressing the many threats they face, not only from the forest-products sector, but also from agriculture, mining, road systems and settlements. **WWF** also advocates the target of 'ZNDD' (zero net deforestation and degradation) by 2020 in response to the urgent need to tackle the threats to both forests and our global climate.

Since this book was first published more than a decade ago, the understanding of and interest in our global ancient tree heritage has grown hugely. Today, there are numerous individuals and organizations all over the world looking for, and campaigning to protect, ancient trees. In the USA, Save the Redwoods League is just one of a number of organizations campaigning for the better protection of America's ancient trees. In China, the University of Hunan has already recorded over 100,000 ancient trees growing in that province alone. In the UK, Europe's largest and most comprehensive public/scientific ancient tree project – the Woodland Trust's Ancient Tree Hunt – had recorded over 100,000 notable trees by the end of 2011. And in tropical South East Asia the ring sequences of old trees are now being recorded, revealing some unexpectedly ancient trees in monsoon countries such as Vietnam – some have been found to have more than 1,000 annual rings. These ring sequences are being studied in order to help our understanding of climatic events in the past.

We are, in many ways, rediscovering our common link with our ancestors through a new respect and reverence for forests and, in particular, for venerable old trees. In a world increasingly dominated by change, these trees provide a tangible link with our past, serving to remind us of the extraordinary antiquity and beauty of life on Earth. This book is intended to be a celebration of some of the world's most ancient trees.

REDWOOD
The phoenix tree

BOTANICAL NAMES
Sequoia sempervirens
(coast redwood)
Sequoiadendron giganteum (giant
redwood)
Metasequoia glyptostroboides
(dawn redwood)

DISTRIBUTION
California, USA and Hubei
Province, China.

OLDEST KNOWN LIVING
SPECIMEN
The giant redwood called General
Sherman is estimated to be 3,269
years old.

RELIGIOUS SIGNIFICANCE
American redwoods are sacred to
the Tolowa people of the Pacific
coast of Oregon and California.

CONSERVATION STATUS
Classified on the IUCN Red
List of Threatened Species in
2006 as follows: coast redwood
'vulnerable'; giant redwood
'vulnerable' and dawn redwood
'critically endangered'.

Imagine standing in a forest of giants, believing that every living thing has a spirit. Imagine looking up at the elegant spires of the coast redwood trees, with their uppermost branches wreathed in mist, towering to over 91m (300ft) above you. Imagine believing that every living thing was made by the supreme Creator under the First Redwood Tree, and that redwoods are the guardians of the streams that provide the food on which you depend – the guardians of your very culture. It may be difficult to appreciate fully the reverence felt by indigenous peoples among these stately giants, but for the Tolowa people of the Pacific coast of California and Oregon, this awareness shaped their world for thousands of years before the arrival of Europeans.

The coast redwood (*Sequoia sempervirens*) that grows today along the Pacific coast of California is a survivor from the forests that covered much of the northern hemisphere 140 million years ago. It is one of three surviving redwood species that retreated to small, isolated areas with specific climatic conditions as the global climate changed. The giant sequoia or redwood (*Sequoiadendron giganteum*) is now restricted to the Sierra Nevada's western slopes in California, while the dawn redwood (*Metasequoia glyptostroboides*) is found only in a remote area of China.

The coast redwoods

The coast redwoods are graceful giants. Able to attain heights of over 91.44m (300ft), they are slim and elegant. Today the tree verified as the world's tallest is a coast redwood known as Hyperion, which stands in Federation Grove in northern California and is 115.61m (379¼ft) in height. This makes it considerably taller than the Statue of Liberty. Its age is estimated at between 2,000 and 3,000 years. The largest coast redwood is the Lost Monarch – a relatively modest 97.8m (321ft) tall, but with a volume of 97.8 cu. m (42,500 cu. ft).

The coast redwood forests are located in a discontinuous belt that runs for 805km (500 miles) along the coasts of northern California and southern Oregon. They are rarely found far from the sea, the furthest stand being just 48km (30 miles) inland, in Napa county. Much of the great redwood forest has now been logged. It is estimated that only 5 per cent of the original coast redwood forest still stands and of this, 82 per cent falls under some sort of protection in forest reserves and parks.

Coast redwoods grow best in areas that have a mild climate and are protected from wind and salt spray. The tallest grow on the flood plains of streams and rivers that are subject to periodic flooding. However, it is the high rainfall – more than 178cm (70in) per year – and summer fogs that have allowed the redwoods to survive for so long in their refuge. The redwoods are unique because they can absorb some moisture through their foliage.

Natural fires are also an important factor in the survival of these last-remaining redwood forests. Redwood seeds have very specific requirements for germination: to be viable they need to be able to reach bare mineral soils, and the

The base of the Tall Tree. one of the world's tallest trees, measured in 1990 at 112m (168ft) high.

fires assist this process by burning away fallen needles and other organic material covering the soil, producing an ash that is rich in nutrients.

The coast redwood has a thick, spongy bark that ranges in colour from reddish-brown to grey. The bark of mature trees may be 15–30cm (6–12in) thick, and its high tannin content makes it resistant to both fire and attacks by fungi and insects.

The redwoods are conifers – that is, cone-bearing trees. The mature cones they produce are reddish-brown in colour, woody and very small. The seeds inside take the form of minute flakes, which drift easily on a light wind, enabling them to disperse. In fact the seeds are so light that 125,000 of them weigh just 0.45 kg

(1 lb). The coast redwoods have a second means of reproduction – by sprouting, or putting out suckers – and are the only cone-bearing trees able to do this.

In their coastal position, the redwoods protect the watersheds of many of the streams and rivers that are important as migratory routes and spawning grounds for salmon and sea trout. The rivers running through areas of mature forest are crystal clear and provide ideal aquatic habitats; where the forests have been removed, the rivers become silted up with soil washed off the denuded slopes.

The role played by the coast redwood forests in the productivity of the rivers was long appreciated by the native peoples who lived – and in some places still live – along the Pacific coast. Before the 'discovery' of North America by Europeans, many different peoples with distinct languages but a common culture inhabited the forested coastlines of California and Oregon. Their societies were based on fishing, hunting and collecting forest produce. The redwoods provided continuity in a dynamic environment – even after catastrophic fires, they would remain standing, protecting the life-giving streams that teemed with fish.

Native peoples along the Pacific coast believed (and still do) that redwoods are an inextricable part of nature, and that respect must be shown to all living things: both plants and animals. For example, whenever plants were gathered, the

In the beginning there was nothing except water and darkness. Then the Creator thought the world into existence. At the centre of the world stood the First Redwood Tree, beneath which were visible the tracks of all animals, which the Creator had also thought into existence. These were pre-humans, which became rocks, trees and animals, and went away when the first people arrived.

THE TOLOWA CREATION MYTH

OPPOSITE
New trees and shrubs are nourished by the trunk of a fallen redwood.

BELOW
A view of part of the Redwood National Park on the Pacific Coast of Northern California.

Life in the canopy

Professor Stephen C. Sillett is a scientist attached to the Institute for Redwood Ecology at Humboldt State University in the USA. He has made a special study of the ecology of tall trees and the forests they create. His remarkable work has given the world a new understanding of what happens high in the canopy of the coast redwood forests, where rare epiphytes and wildlife survive in the delicate microclimates created in the crowns. Professor Sillett is also the only person who has climbed to the top of the five tallest tree species in the world, each rising to over 91.44m (300ft). The tallest tree he has scaled is a coast redwood of 115m (377¼ft), where he discovered an unexpectedly rich community of plant and animal life.

Kashaya Pomo people, who occupied the land in what is now Sonoma county (just north of San Francisco), offered a prayer to their supreme Creator, explaining why the plants were being taken. A special song was sung to the earth spirit to ward off evil; some form of personal sacrifice was also made – perhaps an offering of food or sharing of the produce collected. Selfishness was considered undesirable social behaviour, eventually leading to personal loss or bad luck.

Only 150 years ago, the redwood forest along the Pacific coast was the home of numerous native peoples, including the Sinkyone, the Kashaya Pomo, the south-western Pomo, the Wappo (Ashochimi), the Mendocino and the Tolawa. The Sinkyone people, who are extinct today, regarded the redwoods as sacred protectors of the whole forest, especially of the streams on which so much else depended. Redwood groves acted as guardians of the spirits of their ancestors, whose sacred burial grounds lay among the giant redwood trees or close to them. Kashaya-speaking peoples still have a detailed understanding of the redwood's botany – their conception of plants and plant communities is analogous to that used by Western botanists. Native peoples used redwood timber for house and boat construction and used other parts of the tree for medicines.

The powerful European culture that arrived with the settlers in the middle of the nineteenth century was based on values that were diametrically opposed to those of the indigenous peoples of the region, many of whom, along with their cultures, became extinct. The magnificent redwood trees, so pivotal to their societies, were felled in vast numbers. In 1999, however, the US government paid a lumber company $480 million in order to save the largest tract of privately owned coastal redwood forest at the time. In the last ten years, a further 2,800 ha. (11 sq. miles) of 'old growth' forest has been purchased from the timber industry.

ABOVE
Kings Canyon National Park in California has the largest remaining grove of ancient giant redwoods.

OPPOSITE
The enormous, almost branchless giant redwood trunks attracted loggers in the nineteenth century.

The giant redwoods

Giant redwoods and their close ancestors have been on the Earth for at least 200 million years and, like their coastal cousins, once formed massive forests which stretched across much of the northern hemisphere. Today they are a truly relict species, occurring only in isolated groves on the western slopes of the Sierra Nevada in California.

Although the largest giant redwood in existence does not hold any records for being the oldest, tallest or broadest tree in the world, nothing can match its sheer volume. The tree known as the General Sherman, named after the famous general of the American Civil War, contains an estimated 1,486 cu. m (52,500 cu. ft) of wood. The largest trunk of any redwood is to be found on an individual called the Boole Tree, situated in the Converse Basin, in Sequoia National Park, which is 34.4m (113ft) in circumference at 1.4m (4½ft) above the ground. Giant redwoods are virtually indestructible because they have fire-resistant bark. In fact, the trees

The distinctive red, fire-resistant bark of redwoods on the Congress Trail in California's Sequoia National Park.

need the clearing effect of forest fires to establish new seedlings successfully. They are also resistant to fungi and wood-boring insects. The main cause of death is being blown over. 'Most of the Sierra's [other] trees die of disease, fungi etc.,' wrote the Scots-born American naturalist John Muir in 1868,' but nothing hurts the Big Tree [the giant redwood]. Barring accidents, it seems to be immortal.'

Today there are just 75 groves of giant redwoods left, concentrated in the Kings Canyon and Sequoia National Parks, with a further three groves located in Yosemite. Where they do appear, the redwood forests seem to be healthy and reproducing well.

Giant redwood groves are found only on the slopes of upland ridges between major river canyons at 1,220–2,440m (4,000–8,000ft) above sea level. Here the climate is characterized by warm, dry summers and sunny winters. The latter are, however, interrupted by infrequent snowstorms, which may last from a few days to a week, leaving several metres of snow. The groves are generally tucked away from areas of high wind, but lightning strikes and thunderbolts are relatively common. Just why the giant redwoods are confined to isolated groves remains a mystery. Not a single tree is found outside these groves, even where the same climatic conditions prevail.

The giant redwood has cinnamon-coloured bark, which may grow to a massive 45cm (18in) thick. Unlike the slim, tapering trunk of the coast redwood, the giant's trunk is conical in shape and has a broad base that can measure over 30.5m (100ft) in circumference. Even at 60m (200ft) above the ground, it can still be more than 6m (20ft) in diameter. Its main branches may grow to more than 2.4m (8ft) wide, making the tree's biggest limbs the size of large trees themselves.

The tree stands on a shallow but widely spreading root-pad, which can be enormous, radiating from the trunk for up to 91.44m (300ft), but seldom reaching down into the earth more than 1.8m (6ft). Giant redwoods reach their maximum height in the first 500 years of their life, after which lateral expansion goes on for up to 3,000 years. It is not clear when a redwood stops expanding, because there is no definite record of any giant redwood dying of old age and they continue to grow indefinitely until a natural disaster, such as a lightning strike or storm-force wind, occurs. In 2011, the General Sherman tree was estimated to be 3,269 years old. However, John Muir claimed to have discovered a stump containing 4,000 rings.

As they age, the crowns of the trees change shape. At ages of up to 500 years, the crown is pointed like a spire, but over time it gradually becomes rounded. Fire damage can cause part of the crown to die, as can lightning strikes.

The giant redwoods start to produce seeds after only a few years of life. Mature trees generate about 600 new cones every year and, since each cone contains several hundred healthy seeds, a tree can produce more than 100,000 seeds annually. The largest giant redwood produces some 10,000 cones and as many as two million seeds each year. However, the cones do not simply fall and release their seeds. This function is often performed unwittingly by the chickaree, or Douglas squirrel,

John Muir

John Muir, the renowned naturalist who spent much time walking in the Sierra Nevada mountains, was awe-struck by these giants. 'There is something wonderfully attractive in this king tree, even when beheld from afar, that draws us to it with indescribable enthusiasm; its superior height and massive, smoothly rounded outlines proclaiming its character in any company; and when one of the oldest attains full stature on some commanding ridge it seems the very god of the woods.'

'The majestic sequoia is here, too, the King of Conifers, the noblest of all the noble race … these colossal trees are as wonderful in fineness of beauty and proportion as in stature – an assemblage of conifers surpassing all that have ever yet been discovered in the forests of the world.'

The General Sherman

The giant redwood tree known as the General Sherman, which stands in the Sequoia National Park in California, is one of the largest living things on Earth. Its statistics are truly impressive – volume 1,486.6 cu. m (52,500 cu. ft), height 83.8m (275ft), and age 3,269 years. Its circumference at ground level is 31.1m (102ft), its trunk measures 7.7m (25ft) in diameter at mean breast height, and it is still 4.3m (14ft) in diameter at 55m (180ft). (Measurements courtesy of the National Park Service.)

which finds the fleshy scales of the cones delicious. As it feeds on them, the seeds are scattered on the forest floor. Once the seeds reach the ground, they will germinate only under exactly the right conditions.

The sugar pines and yellow pines that (along with the redwoods) form the mixed conifer forests of the Sierra Nevada rely on fire to create gaps in the overhead canopy and clear the forest floor. The fires also dry the redwood cones on higher branches, which then release their seeds on to the cooling ashes below. The action of the fires allows the seeds to fall on areas of bare mineral soil, where the sunlight is able to filter through. Where fires have been prevented, the forest floor rapidly becomes colonized by shade-tolerant white firs and incense cedars, hindering redwood regeneration.

The birth of the giant redwood has been likened to the rising from the ashes of the fabulous mythical bird, the phoenix, which eternally renews itself and has thereby become a symbol of immortality.

The dawn redwoods

The discovery of the deciduous dawn redwood (*Metasequoia glyptostroboides*) in China in 1941 made headlines across the world. Described as a 'living fossil', it was identified as one of the ancient relatives of the redwoods in California. Until 1941 it had only been known from Japanese fossil specimens dating back between 1.5 and 6 million years.

The first specimen seen by an outsider stood in the remote village of Madoaoqui in the western part of Hubei province. At its base was a small shrine, to which local people brought offerings. Later, a whole forest of dawn redwoods was found less than 48km (30 miles) away in the Valley of the Tiger, near Shui-se-pa.

The Bureau of Forestry in the province of Lichuan Xian keeps a census of all the dawn redwoods in the area. Today there are believed to be around 6,000 mature seed-producing trees, several of which are over 50m (164ft) tall. However, despite being adopted by the Chinese as almost a national tree, with seedlings being planted in great numbers, these fast-growing trees are still considered critically endangered in the wild.

OPPOSITE
A fine example of a dawn redwood – a species once thought to have become extinct millions of years ago – with its distinctive tapering trunk.

BRISTLECONE PINE
The tree that rewrote history

BOTANICAL NAME
Pinus longaeva (Great Basin bristlecone pine); *Pinus aristata* (Rocky Mountain bristlecone pine)

DISTRIBUTION
California, Nevada and Utah, USA.

OLDEST KNOWN LIVING SPECIMEN
The Methuselah Tree in California: over 4,600 years old.

HISTORICAL SIGNIFICANCE
Known as the 'tree that rewrote history' because it provided wood with a tree-ring chronology spanning 8,000 years, allowing the carbon-14 dating technique to be accurately calibrated.

CONSERVATION STATUS
Classified on the IUCN Red List of Threatened Species in 2011 as of 'least concern'.

On a barren mountainside in eastern California's White Mountains, a grove of ancient pine trees clings to life. Bleached by the sun, smoothed by the corrosive force of fierce winds bearing sand and ice, these Great Basin bristlecone pines (*Pinus longaeva*) have been moulded into grotesque natural sculptures by their inhospitable environment. Undistinguished by size or beauty, these strange trees are, however, incredibly old, and are thought to be able to reach ages of over 5,000 years. Here stand the Schulman Grove and the famous Methuselah Tree, which has a verifiable age of over 4,600 years according to carbon-dating research. It was named by Dr Edward Schulman in 1957, after the Hebrew patriarch of the Old Testament whose long lifespan has made him a byword for longevity.

Looking out across an environment that has remained almost unchanged for more than 10,000 years, it seems possible to step outside time and share a moment of silence with these living organisms, which began their lives before the great pyramids of Egypt were constructed. Even before the rise of the great empires of the Greeks, Mayans and Romans, the Methuselah Tree was already one of Earth's elder statesmen.

A hostile environment

Two species of bristlecone pine exist. Though growing only 260km (160 miles) apart, those found on the high ridges of the Great Basin country (extending from the eastern border of California across Nevada to Utah) reach the greatest age. The Rocky Mountain bristlecone pines (*Pinus aristata*), which reach ages of up to 1,500 years, are to be found in an area that extends from the eastern slopes of the southern Rocky Mountains in Wyoming through Colorado and down into New Mexico. The environment in which the bristlecone pines live seems an unlikely place in which to find trees of such antiquity. In fact, it is the very harshness of this environment, and the bristlecone's response to it, that have enabled the tree to achieve such a great age.

The Great Basin bristlecone pines grow on steep, rocky slopes at an altitude of 2,750–3,500m (9,000–11,500ft) above sea level. Between November and

April each year, temperatures plummet to well below freezing and the area may receive 2.7m (9ft) of snow. These conditions are exacerbated by the ferocious winds that scour the mountainsides. The bristlecone pine has adapted by lengthening its growing season and by putting on new growth when temperatures are much too cold for other plants.

Most of the trees are under 9m (30ft) tall, and much of their wood – on the windward side, at least – is dead. The sparse crowns of twisted and contorted branches are supported only by narrow strips of living wood. The ability of the bristlecone to live in nutrient-poor soils and to conserve water has been vital to the survival of the species. The tree has developed special waxy leaves (needles), which may not be shed for over 20 years, thus helping to reduce evaporation and conserve moisture; it also contains high levels of resin, which acts as a wood preservative and which is exuded to form a waterproof layer over any exposed branches. To maximize water absorption, the tree also has an extensive network of shallow roots.

The arid conditions in which bristlecone pines live means that timber from fallen trees can lie on the ground without decomposing for thousands of years.

Evidence that the great longevity of the trees is directly related to the harshness of their environment is provided by the fact that the average age of bristlecone pines on south-facing slopes in the White Mountains is typically around 1,000 years, whereas on north-facing slopes, the average age rises to over 2,000 years. Entire groves of trees that are over 4,000 years old stand on the north-facing slopes, and it is amid one of these groves that the ancient Methuselah Tree is found. The appearance of bristlecone forest on north- and south-facing slopes is markedly different. While the southern slopes have many healthy-looking trees, covering the hillside in quite dense forests, north-facing slopes contain trees that are much more widely spaced, squat and gnarled, with many dead branches. The severity of the environment on the north-facing slopes causes the growth rings to be more tightly packed, which in turn makes the timber more durable and the trees longer-lived. The durability of the timber is so exceptional that scientists have found dead wood, which, amazingly, has been shown to be over 8,000 years old, lying intact close to living trees.

A forest consisting of trees that are thousands of years old can afford to regenerate at a leisurely pace. Only a handful of new seedlings need to germinate successfully each century to ensure the forest's survival. Bristlecone pines are found in pure stands but often form communities with limber pines (*Pinus flexilis*) and other tree species, as well as understorey plants such as sage

The Prometheus Tree

In 1964 Donald R. Currey, an undergraduate researcher, asked the US Forest Service if he could cut down one tree – to study the annual growth rings of bristlecone pines growing in a grove beneath Wheeler Peak. The Forest Service agreed, but unfortunately the tree he cut down revealed later that it had no fewer than 4,862 rings and a hollow core, which meant that it had probably been growing for over 5,000 years and was several hundred years older than the oldest still growing today. It became known as the Prometheus Tree, a name from Ancient Greek myth: Prometheus brought fire (symbolic of knowledge) to humans.

Despite the tragedy of the felling of the world's oldest verifiable living organism, the knowledge gained from studying it has added to the scientific understanding of carbon dating and climate change over the past 11,000 years.

brushes (*Artemisia spp.*), wax currant (*Ribes cereum*) and curl-leaf mountain mahogany (*Cercocarpus ledifolius*). Birds such as the mountain bluebird, the chickadee and Clark's nutcracker feed on their seeds. The latter is most important for the bristlecone pine's regeneration, because it collects seeds and buries them in caches in the soil, thus helping the seedlings to gain a foothold in the inhospitable terrain.

Verifying the past

Because bristlecone pine wood is extremely durable and can survive intact for thousands of years, scientists have been able to look not only at the ring sequences of living trees, but at those of dead trees that have remained preserved on the ground. This fact enabled a highly significant breakthrough to be made in the science of radiocarbon-dating archaeological artefacts. During the late 1950s, the study of tree rings, using wood that was dated to the exact year of its formation, enabled scientists to confirm the discrepancy between the radiocarbon ages and actual calendar ages of objects containing carbon, and recalibrate their method of measurement. It was found that many objects were 1,000 years older than previously thought.

In the 1960s, the overlapping of living ring sequences with those of dead trees enabled the first calibration curve based on a continuous tree-ring sequence stretching back more than 8,000 years to be constructed. This research also revealed valuable information about the climatic conditions of the past. Tree rings are still used today to calibrate radiocarbon measurements and tree-ring libraries representing different calendar ages are now available, providing records that go back over 11,000 years. While trees such as the waterlogged oak (*Quercus* spp.) are also used, the enormous significance of data obtained from the bristlecone pine has justified its name as the 'tree that rewrote history'.

Bristlecones are able to reduce their energy requirements for living to a very low level by shedding their branches and allowing parts of the tree to die back. They rarely exceed 9m (30ft) in height but their timber is remarkably dense and durable.

OPPOSITE
The wind-sculpted trunk of a living Bristlecone pine in the Methuselah Grove high in the White Mountains. Over time, the harsh climatic conditions turn many ancient trees into striking organic sculptures.

MONTEZUMA BALD CYPRESS
Swamp giant

BOTANICAL NAME
Taxodium mucronatum

DISTRIBUTION
Often near rivers, springs, marshes
or former swampland: widespread
and locally common in Mexico;
rare and localized in Guatemala;
a few examples in Texas, USA,
where it is in danger of extinction.

**OLDEST KNOWN
LIVING SPECIMEN**
The tree known as El Tule,
growing at Santa Maria del Tule,
near Oaxaca, Mexico: 36.3m
(119ft) in girth, or 53.7m (176ft)
including irregularities at 1m
(3¼ft) from the ground; estimated
age: 1,200–3,000 years old.

RELIGIOUS SIGNIFICANCE
Sacred to the ancient peoples
of Mexico.

MYTHICAL ASSOCIATIONS
Linked to Zapotec origin myths.

CONSERVATION STATUS
Classified on the IUCN Red List of
Threatened Species in 2011 as of
'least concern'.

The Montezuma bald cypress known as El Tule is an astonishing tree. To stand before it and look up into its crown is like looking at a living version of Notre Dame Cathedral. Its fluted bole is reminiscent of the flying buttresses that support this architectural masterpiece. Both are immense; both demand the same degree of reverence and awe. El Tule is to be found near the village that has taken its name from the tree: Santa Maria del Tule, some 14km (9 miles) from the town of Oaxaca, in southern Mexico. Also known as the ahuehuete, the Montezuma bald cypress (*Taxodium mucronatum*) is a species that grows almost exclusively in Mexico.

Some botanists consider this to be the same species as the tree known as the swamp, southern or bald cypress (classified as *Taxodium distichum*), which is found in the south-eastern United States and grows in a similar habitat. Recognition of its colossal size, beauty and longevity led to its official recognition as the National Tree of Mexico in 1921 and various ancient individual specimens are protected as 'monuments'.

Montezuma bald cypresses generally grow to a height of 20–30m (65–100ft), but can exceed 35m (115ft). El Tule is the largest individual in Mexico, but it is not actually the tallest; other giant trees also exist. A tree standing in Mexico City's Chapultepec Park was recorded, using a laser, as being 37.8m (124ft) high, making it the tallest.

The tree is an evergreen, but in the winter and spring months the foliage can appear a rusty-red colour as the new leaf buds develop. An interesting feature of these slow-growing giants is the apparent tendency of their massive, fluted and burr-covered boles to split as they grow, giving the impression, in old age, that they are not one but several trees joined together. This can be a complicating factor when trying to estimate the age of ancient trees. The distinguished Mexican botanist Maximíno Martinez, founder of Mexico's Botanical Society, who made a detailed study of the country's Montezuma bald cypresses, concluded in the 1950s that trees such as El Tule were not the result of a fusion of separate individuals, but of the division of the main trunk at its base. DNA studies undertaken in 1996 also confirmed that it is in fact a single tree.

The Montezuma bald cypress produces new foliage that is a rusty-red in colour.

El Tule – the fissured giant

In his *Historia Natural y Moral de las Indias* of 1586, the Spanish chronicler José Acosta noted that according to the local Zapotec Indians, El Tule was a truly colossal tree some 100 years earlier, able to provide shade for 1,000 people. Though the exact date is not known, at some point during the fifteenth century it was struck by lightning, which ripped the tree asunder leaving a huge hollow, while reducing the magnificent crown to a mass of splintered branches and tattered foliage.

When the first Europeans arrived in the Mexican state of Oaxaca, where El Tule stands, it was still an impressive sight. Acosta, who provided the first written record of it, described it as a huge shell of a tree, which measured 16 arm's lengths (a little under 27m/89ft) near its base, which was split into three sections. In a letter written on 7 March 1630, the Spanish priest Bernabé Cobo described the tree as follows:

'Amongst the ruins of the old village, there is a hollow tree so wide at its base, that it looks as if it would make a very capacious dwelling; it has three entrances that are so huge that you can ride through them on horseback, and there is room inside for 12 horsemen; four of us who came rode in on our horses and there was still room for another eight, I measured it outside having brought with me a ball of thread for the purpose, and it measured round its base 26 varas [17.5m/57ft]; … it is alive, still with many branches and leaves, although years ago a lightning strike damaged most of its branches. From here to the town of Oaxaca it is three leagues …'

Almost 400 years later, the tree has risen again. The gaping hollow – estimated to have been some 12–18 sq. m (129–93 sq. ft) in size – has been filled with new timber, and the regenerating branches have become mighty boughs that support a

All was darkness when the Zapotecs were born. They burst forth from the old trees, like the ceiba (and El Tule) from the stomachs of the wild beasts they were born, like the jaguar and the lizard.

ZAPOTEC ORIGIN MYTH

During the seventeenth century the hollow inside El Tule was reputed to have been large enough to be able to hold twelve men on horseback.

dome of foliage some 44m (144ft) across, rising to a height of almost 35m (114ft). It is now one of the world's greatest trees, with a bole measuring 36.3m (119ft) round at breast height or 53.7m (176ft), including all the irregularities of the gnarled and buttressed trunk.

The exact age of El Tule is unknown, with estimates ranging from between 1,200 and 3,000 years old. The best scientific estimate, based on growth rates, is 1,433–1,600 years old. Interestingly, there is a local Zapotec legend that states that it was planted about 1,400 years ago by Pechocha, a priest of Ehecatl, the Aztec wind god, which is very much in line with the scientific estimate. Further north, near San Luis Potosi, is a group of ahuehutes, the largest of which is just 22m (72ft) tall and 2m (6½ft) in diameter. Core sample analysis has shown that one of the trees in this group has a confirmed age of 1,140 years. El Tule has a diameter approximately five times greater than this 1,000-year-old tree, which is why some people are tempted to suggest that it is one of the oldest trees on Earth.

Ancient name, ancient environment

The native Zapotec Indians who were living in the vicinity of El Tule when the Spanish conquistadores arrived in the early sixteenth century called the site Luguiaga (later renamed Santa María by the Spanish), which has been roughly translated as 'amongst the reeds'. This name provides evidence to support the descriptions made by early Spanish observers of the local environment: that it was a large, reed-filled swamp, or certainly flooded for much of the time.

Before the arrival of the Spanish in Mexico the lingua franca in Mesoamerica was Nahuatl – the language of the ruling Aztecs, whose last emperor was the distinguished warrior Montezuma II (1466–1520), from whom the Montezuma bald cypress takes its name. Luguiaga was also known, more widely, by its Nahuatl name of Tollin or Tullin. This is a generic term for aquatic plants, and it evolved into the hispanicized word *tule*. The term still used today for all Montezuma bald cypresses, *ahuehuete*, is also a Nahuatl word meaning, in Spanish, *viejos de agua* – literally, 'ancients of the water'. Indeed, the trees naturally occur next to rivers, streams, springs or swampy ground and the roots have adapted by producing pneumatophores or 'breathing roots'.

It is interesting then, to note that El Tule and other large Montezuma bald cypresses are now found in locations that are distinctly arid, bearing testament to the fact that much of Mexico has become desertified over the last 2,000 years. That El Tule began its life in a swamp or on the edge of a lake or river seems certain, but it has had to depend upon water drawn from very deep down, by its network of roots, in order to survive. Since 1952, to help compensate for the increasing scarcity of underground water, the survival of the tree has been assisted by the installation of an underground irrigation system designed to water its roots.

As is recorded at the National Museum of Anthropology in Mexico City, the ancient Aztec people, the Mexica, took advantage of the Montezuma bald cypress's demand for large amounts of water and the ability of its roots to bind rocks and soil together, and put it to very practical use. By planting trees in the form of palisades within shallow lakes and filling the spaces in between with earth, wetlands could gradually be drained and turned into land suitable for growing crops. This was done around the once extensive Lake Texcoco, on which the Aztec city of Tenochtitlán was built – now the site of the vast Mexico City.

El Tule was a great tree during the period in which one of the most advanced empires in the world, that of the Aztecs, was at its peak; in some ways it is symbolic of the history of Mexico's native peoples who have, despite adversity, managed to survive. Today El Tule stands proud: not just as part of Mexico's history, but as an integral part of its future.

MONKEY PUZZLE
Tree of fire and ice

BOTANICAL NAME
Araucaria araucana

DISTRIBUTION
Today restricted to two small areas along the coast of central Chile and a larger area in the Cordillera of the Andes, on the borders of Chile and Argentina.

OLDEST-KNOWN LIVING SPECIMEN
Approximately 2,000 years old — no exact location known.

RELIGIOUS SIGNIFICANCE
Sacred to the Pehuenche people of south-central Chile, who regard it as a 'mother'. They believe that God created monkey puzzle trees for them, and that it is their duty to protect them. Also a national monument of Chile.

CONSERVATION STATUS
Classified on the IUCN Red List of Threatened Species in 2000 as 'vulnerable – facing a high risk of extinction in the wild'.

The monkey puzzle, with its strangely prehistoric shape, is an extraordinary tree. Many fine specimens can be seen gracing gardens and parks around the world, but their true home is the volcanic slopes of the high Andes mountains of southern South America. Here the monkey puzzle thrives in an inhospitable terrain. Amid volcanic debris, and often clinging to precipitous slopes and the crests of hills, it seems impervious to the extremes of heat, cold and hurricane-force winds. The trees are adapted to the harshest of living conditions, including volcanic eruptions and heavy falls of winter snow.

Living fossils

Sometimes referred to as living fossils, monkey puzzles (*Araucaria araucana*) have an extremely ancient heritage. Remains of trees belonging to the same family have been found, fossilized, in rocks that were formed during the Jurassic period, some 225 million years ago. About 190 million years ago, the trees were one of the dominant species of the southern hemisphere, with a range that stretched from

Brazil to Antarctica. Today, however, monkey puzzles are found in only a very restricted region: two small areas in the Cordillera of Nahuelbuta along the coast of central Chile, and a larger area in the Cordillera of the Andes on the borders of Chile and Argentina. Preferring north- and west-facing slopes, they grow primarily on volcanic soils, about 600–1,800m (2,000–6,000ft) above sea level. The trees grow both in pure stands and in association with other trees, notably species of southern beech (*Nothofagus* spp.).

While young monkey puzzles resemble a pyramid or cone in shape until they begin to lose their lower branches, at about 100 years old, mature trees are distinguished by their well-defined crown, which develops some 18–30m (60–100ft) above the ground, giving them the appearance of an open umbrella.

The rosette formation of spiky leaves at the tip of a monkey puzzle branch.

The monkey's puzzle

Monkey puzzles can live to a great age. It is not uncommon to find individuals of over 1,300 years old; the oldest are believed to be around 2,000 years old. Growing very slowly, mature monkey puzzles develop perfectly straight, column-like trunks, which can reach some 50m (165ft) in height and measure 2.5m (8ft) in diameter at breast height. The trees also develop a remarkable bark with a fascinating honeycomb pattern. In mature trees, the bark can be up to 18cm (7in) thick and may account for up to 25 per cent of the trunk's volume. It plays an important role in protecting the tree from the extremes of the Andean climate and, importantly, is able to resist the intense heat of volcanic eruptions.

Like the bark, the curious triangular leaves of the monkey puzzle are extremely tough. They are arranged in spirals and are attached directly to the twigs and branches of the trees, and to the young trunk in early life. It is the curious arrangement of leaves and branches that was responsible for the tree's common name of 'monkey puzzler', which came into use during the late nineteenth century. Although monkeys did not live in the forests of Chile, early European observers thought that the trees would present any monkey with a challenge! According to Maud Woodcock, writing in the 1940s, 'The monkey's puzzle consists in the monkey being able to go up the sharp points of the tree but not down them'.

While they do not support monkeys, the trees do provide the habitat for a number of rare and endangered animals. These include the puma, the Chilean pigeon and the slender-billed parakeet. One of the principal foods of the parakeet is the seed, produced by the female monkey puzzle tree, inside cones that can grow to the size of a person's head. Individual cones may contain about 200 tapering seeds, each about 4cm (1½in.) long. Though they consume many seeds, the parakeets also play a part in their distribution – as they force their sharp beaks inside the cones, the cones split, releasing the seeds, which fall to the ground. The existence of certain dense groupings of monkey puzzle trees is said to be due to the activity of mole rats, which also inhabit the Chilean forests and bury quantities of seeds each year.

The Pehuenche – people of the monkey puzzles

It is the connection between monkey puzzle trees and people that is perhaps the most significant aspect of their existence. One of South America's native peoples takes its name directly from the tree, since their culture and identity have been shaped by it. These people are the Pehuenche, whose name means 'people of the monkey puzzles' – from *pehuen*, meaning 'monkey puzzle', and *che*, meaning 'people'. About 5,000 Pehuenche people currently live in the valley of the upper Bio-Bio, the longest river in the south-central region of Chile. The Pehuenche are traditionally a resilient and independent people – part of the great Mapuche nation, the indigenous population of half the area that is today known as Argentina and Chile, whom the Incas never managed to conquer and who remained beyond the control of both the Chilean and Argentinian republics until just over 100 years ago.

For part of each year, during late summer and early autumn, the Pehuenche live mainly as food-gatherers in the upland volcanic forests, collecting the

ABOVE
Monkey puzzles' fire-resistant bark can be 18cm (7in) thick, helping them survive the eruptions of active volcanoes in the Chilean Andes.

OPPOSITE
A Pehuenche man on horseback, in the bitter winter conditions that occur high in the Andes.

BELOW
Monkey puzzle seeds (*piñones*) are an essential part of the Pehuenche diet.

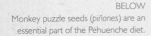

nutritious monkey puzzle seeds. These golden-brown seeds, known as *piñones* in Spanish, are the Pehuenche's traditional staple food. They are gathered both for immediate consumption and for storage, to be eaten throughout the year, forming the main source of carbohydrate during the long winter from June to September. The harvesting of *piñones* is a skilful job. Some seeds will be picked up from the ground where they have fallen naturally, but Pehuenche men also scale the trees with the aid of ropes, carrying long, thin poles with which to knock down more seeds. They strike the ripe cones, which usually shatter when they are hit, sending showers of seeds falling to the ground, where women and children quickly gather them. Large numbers of piñones are often gathered during the harvest: a single

family may be able to collect as much as **3,000kg (6,630lb)** of seeds each year, although in some years the trees produce smaller quantities. The Pehuenche are careful, however, not to knock down all the cones from the trees or collect all the seeds from the ground, mindful that enough must be left to allow regeneration.

Piñones are similar to sweet chestnuts in texture and taste and are generally boiled or roasted, after which the tough outer skin is removed. They may also be ground into a coarse flour used in soups and for making bread, or turned into a nutritious fermented drink. Monkey puzzle seeds are fed to animals, too. The Pehuenche once obtained their meat by hunting wild guanaco, a relative of the domesticated llama, but today they tend to keep small numbers of sheep and goats, and the occasional horse. During the long, harsh winters, when nearly **2m (6ft)** of snow can cut off some of the remoter communities from the outside world, *piñones* form a useful animal feed.

Many families also sell a proportion of the seed harvest to traders, who may travel long distances to buy direct from the Pehuenche. The piñones are then resold in lowland towns and in regional and provincial capitals, as well as the national capitals, Santiago and Buenos Aires. The Pehuenche are generally paid very little for the seeds, but the money that they generate is vital to enable them to buy many of the goods they need, including clothing and items of hardware, from nearby villages and towns.

Trees with a spirit

The monkey puzzle tree is like a mother to the Pehuenche. It is sacred, revered and respected. They may speak to it, bless it and pray to it in the course of their daily lives. The Pehuenche regard the monkey puzzle forest as part of their extended family, or *lofpehuen*, and as the origin of their own ancestry. The male tree, *wentrupehuen*, and the female tree, *domopehuen*, are believed to reproduce through the connection of their extensive root system, while two old trees are thought to protect the forests. Before the harvest begins, Pehuenche communities traditionally perform a special ceremony in order to ask permission to collect the seeds and ensure that the harvest will be good. A particular tree is selected, around which special prayers are said. This young tree is seen as a magical bridge between

The monkey puzzle is our tree. It's a symbol for us. It's a tree that God left on Earth, for us, the Pehuenche. We cannot cut it down, because it gives us our daily bread. In the end, we would rather die than give up defending this tree.

ALFREDO MELINIR (*LONQO* OR CHIEF OF THE PEHUENCHE COMMUNITY NEAR LONQUIMAY), 1996

OPPOSITE
A magnificent stand of monkey puzzles on the slopes of the Lonquimay Volcano in south central Chile.

Earth and the cosmos beyond. Some Pehuenche make a pilgrimage every year to the site of one particular sacred monkey puzzle tree located north of the Bio-Bio River.

The Pehuenche believe that everything, including the forest, has its own spirit, or *pulli*, and that an equilibrium exists in nature that should not be upset by human beings. Although pieces of old dead wood – often found where the branches protrude from the trunk – are used as firewood, to fell a monkey puzzle would be unthinkable to them.

The battle to save the trees

Since the 1800s, the monkey puzzle forests of Chile and Argentina have been over-exploited by national and international businesses. The timber has been used for many purposes including the construction of train rails, tunnels, ship masts, aeroplane bodies, ceilings, floorings, furniture, pianos, skis, beams for mine construction and, in recent years, to produce cellulose for paper pulp. Logging has not only been carried out without the consent of the Pehuenche or the acknowledgement of their traditional lands, but also largely without reforestation. Today deforested areas have been mostly replaced by farmland or plantations of rapidly growing exotic trees such as eucalyptus.

Monkey puzzle trees are protected under Appendix I of CITES (Convention on International Trade in Endangered Species of Wild Fauna and Flora) and in Chile felling has also (since 1990) been banned other than for scientific purposes. The monkey puzzle is also the national tree of Chile. However, the species is facing a high risk of extinction in the wild because of a severely reduced and fragmented distribution, and the fact that trees continue to be felled illegally both inside and outside national parks. This view is supported by data gathered by the UN Environment Programme World Conservation Monitoring Centre, which analysed satellite images of monkey puzzle forests as far back as 1977. It found that by the first few years of the twenty-first century (2003), the forest had been reduced by 64 per cent and that the remaining forest has become highly fragmented.

Mature monkey puzzles have evolved to withstand fire and to be able to regenerate, given time, from seedlings or root suckers. However, a series of serious fires in recent decades, which appear to have been started in suspicious circumstances and which have given loggers an excuse to clear large areas of burnt trees, have been the cause of much forest loss. Major fires broke out on Pehuenche land near the small town of Lonquimay during the 1990s, incensing the local people. Ricardo Meliñir, the *lonqo* or spiritual leader of the community of Quinquén, said at the time: 'After all these years defending the trees, it's a scandal. We want people everywhere to know what has happened here.' More fires, reported to have destroyed nearly 30,000 ha (115 sq. miles) of native forest, occurred in the

summer season of 2001–2002. The worst-affected area was the Malleco National Reserve, which saw 71 per cent of the *Araucaria* forest destroyed. A number of individual trees were believed to have been more than 2,000 years old.

Over the years, groups of Pehuenche from many different locations have tried to stop the depletion of monkey puzzle forests by timber traders. Since 1976, efforts to protect the remaining forests have been also been attempted by CONAF (Cooporación Nacional Forestal), with the setting up of national reserves, but the restrictions placed on the movements and activities of the Pehuenche have led to considerable tensions and problems. International NGOs have tried to assist, but projects have tended to not fully appreciate the enormous and profound knowledge that Pehuenche people themselves have with regard to the management of their forest.

In response to what has been regarded as inappropriate outside help, different villages and groups of Pehuenche have formed indigenous organizations, such as the Associación Indígena Mapuche Pewenche de Ikalma 'Markan Kura', formed in 2001. They have undertaken a variety of projects, communally, to enhance biodiversity (such as the reforestation of degraded areas), based on indigenous knowledge and which respect their own cultural identity. This model of conservation respects the fact that the Pehuenche have profound ecological knowledge based on centuries of natural resource management.

Like so many other indigenous peoples worldwide, the Pehuenche have suffered badly from the repeated refusal of others to respect their rights and their ancestral land. Much of the extensive monkey puzzle forests that once supported them has been destroyed. But the Pehuenche are a proud and tenacious people and it is largely due to their efforts that monkey puzzles remain today.

RIGHT
A Pehuenche man in an area of destroyed monkey puzzle forest near Lonquimay.

OPPOSITE
Monkey puzzle trees thrive in an inhospitable climate, and can survive extremes of heat in summer as well as heavy falls of winter snow.

AMAZONIAN ANCIENTS
Five survivors

BOTANICAL NAMES
Bertholletia excelsa (Brazil nut);
Cariniana micrantha (castanha
de macaco); *Dipteryx odorata*
(cumaru); *Hymenolobium* spp.
(angelim da mata); *Manilkara
huberi* (maçaranduba)

DISTRIBUTION
Parts of the Amazon rainforest.

**OLDEST KNOWN LIVING
SPECIMEN**
Castanha de macaco: up to
1,400 years old.

MYTHICAL ASSOCIATIONS
Ancient trees in general play a
significant role in Amerindian
origin myths.

CONSERVATION STATUS
On the IUCN Red List of
Threatened Species: Brazil nut
classified as 'vulnerable'
in 1998, and Cumaru as
'vulnerable' (1994).

For many centuries the great Amazon rainforest of Brazil has inspired awe and respect in all who have experienced its wonders at first hand. Charles Darwin (1809–82) wrote: 'Delight … is a weak term to express the feelings of a naturalist who, for the first time, has wandered by himself in a Brazilian forest … the beauty of the flowers, the glossy green of the foliage, but, above all, the general luxuriance of the vegetation filled me with admiration.'

The pioneering studies of naturalists and explorers such as Alexander von Humboldt (1769–1859), Alfred Wallace (1823–1913) and Henry Walter Bates (1825–92) helped to reveal Amazonia's fantastic natural wealth. Yet today, despite the great volume of scientific research that has taken place in recent times, the Amazon continues to be an enigmatic and mysterious place that holds many secrets. Though much continues to be degraded or destroyed – chiefly by large-scale farming, logging, mining, road and dam construction – a mosaic of highly diverse forest still conceals Amerindian peoples who have managed to avoid direct contact with the modern world, and countless species of plant and insect are still unknown to Western science; until recently, it was not realized that many of its great trees could live for over 1,000 years.

The discovery of Amazonia's ancients

For many years it was considered unlikely that any Amazonian tree could live to a great age because of the accelerated rates of growth and decay that occur in the rainforest. However, research carried out during the late 1990s, in forest near the Amazonian city of Manaus, revolutionized our understanding not just of ancient Amazonian trees, but also of the timescale of the ecological cycles of which they are a part.

It has been difficult to assess the true age of Amazonian trees because many do not exhibit the characteristic tree rings that most species native to temperate forests display. Tree rings are formed as a result of the growth put on during a distinct growing season. As the seasons in the Amazon are less clearly defined than those in temperate regions, in many species annual rings are irregular or do not exist at all. With this in mind, Niro Higuchi (of the Instituto Nacional de Pesquisas in Manaus), Jeffrey Chambers and Joshua Schimel (of the Department of Ecology at the University of California, Santa Barbara) decided to use radiocarbon-dating methods to assess the age of tree stumps left behind by a large logging operation

I could only wonder at the sombre shades, scarce illuminated by a single direct ray of the sun, the enormous size and height of the trees, most of which rise in huge columns 100ft [30m] or more without throwing out a single branch; the furrowed stems of others; the extraordinary creepers which wind around them, hanging in long festoons from branch to branch, sometimes curling and twisting on the ground like great serpents, then sprouting to the very tops of the trees, thence throwing lower roots and fibres which hang waving in the air, or twisting round each other to form ropes and cables of every variety and size.

ALFRED RUSSEL WALLACE, *TRAVELS ON THE AMAZON AND RIO NEGRO,* 1889

OPPOSITE
A Euglossine bee on a rainforest orchid.

BELOW
Magnificent castanha de macaco trees like this one can live for at least 1,400 years.

near Manaus. This method revealed the remarkable fact that at least four tree species native to the Amazon can live to over 1,000 years of age: the castanha de macaco (*Cariniana micrantha*), the cumaru (*Dipteryx odorata*), the angelim da mata (*Hymenolobium spp.*) and the maçaranduba (*Manilkara huberi*). A total of 20 trees from 13 different species were studied and their ages were established to range between 200 and 1,400 years, the oldest of these being the cumaru and castanha de macaco.

Another *Cariniana* species may reach an even greater age. Recent studies of trees in a section of the Atlantic Forest of eastern Brazil have led scientists to estimate that one giant example of *Cariniana legalis* that towers over the surrounding forest may possibly be over 2,000 years old.

Of the 15 species of *Cariniana* native to South America, the castanha de macaco or 'monkey nut', which is related to the Brazil nut, produces – as it its name suggests – fruits that are relished in particular by monkeys. The castanha de macaco is a tall, emergent tree whose foliage forms a pale green dome that rises above the surrounding canopy. The elegant cumaru, with its distinctive mottled grey and salmon-coloured bark is, like the castanha de macaco, a prized timber tree. It is also the source of tonka beans. Developing from the tree's eye-catching purple flowers, and with a distinctive odour of new-mown hay, these beans were once widely used in Europe as a tonic and aromatic, because of the compound – coumarin – that they contain. They are still used for flavouring and perfumery today.

The maçaranduba (*Manilkara huberi*), which can reach 40m (131ft) or more in height, is interesting in a different way. It is one of a number of trees that have continued to intrigue many visitors to Amazonia – at least since the time of explorers such as Alexander von Humboldt and Richard Spruce (1817–93) – who

Million-dollar bees

Beautiful iridescent bees provide a service worth millions of dollars to the economies of Bolivia and Brazil. Female euglossine and other vigorous bees that are able to push themselves inside the flowers of the Brazil nut tree are its main pollinators. Euglossine bees, however, are dependent upon particular rainforest orchids to help them reproduce: the male bees collect the scent produced by the orchids and this is released at display sites to help attract females. Although Brazil nut trees are protected by law, large areas of forest continue to be cleared around them, destroying the orchids and the pollinating insects vital for their survival. It is for this reason that the trees cannot be successfully grown in plantations: with no pollinating agents Brazil nuts will not be produced. This is just one way in which deforestation poses a major threat to the local economy.

Mythology

Many Amerindian myths exist about the Creator causing great winds, devastating fires and floods, which may be linked to the influence of El Niño. A myth of the Urubu people of northern Brazil, for example, tells how the Creator, Mair, set fire to the world and then put out the flames with a flood. Large and ancient trees are also traditionally important to Amazonian Indians. Most indigenous groups have an intimate knowledge of the variation within species that exists locally, and also an understanding of the ages of particular ancient trees. A large or ancient tree is a recurring theme in Amerindian origin myths: either the Creator or the first people often emerge from such trees. In Urubu myths, the Creator emerges from a Jatoba tree. The vulture emerges from the pau d'arco, and people come from the *wira pitang* or redwood tree.

Perhaps no country in the world contains such an amount of vegetable matter on its surface as the valley of the Amazon. Its entire extent, with the exception of some very small portions, is covered with one dense and lofty primeval forest, the most extensive and unbroken which exists upon the Earth.

ALFRED RUSSEL WALLACE, *TRAVELS ON THE AMAZON AND RIO NEGRO*, 1889

Latex collected from maçaranduba trees was once widely used to make chewing gum. Trees have also been widely felled for their timber.

noticed that the white, sweetish-tasting latex that oozed from the bark when cut could be drunk like milk, without any harmful effects.

The angelim da mata is one of ten *Hymenolobium* species. It is distinguished by its beautiful flaking bark – a deep red in colour – and by its pink or magenta flowers. The tree's seeds have a delicate, papery surround, which enables them to float to the ground.

The best known of Amazonia's ancient trees, however, is the Brazil nut (*Bertholletia excelsa*), which occurs across a wide area of the Amazon. A magnificent tree, its distinctive silhouette can be seen rising to heights of over 50m (164ft) in the rainforest. Many groves of mature Brazil nut trees in the Amazon today were planted long ago by Amazonian Indians. Indeed, it is now recognized that the distribution of many of Amazonia's trees, and the forest's very diversity, is due in part to human activity over very long periods of time. When Chambers, Schimel and Higuchi carried out their pioneering research, the Brazil nut was at that time the only tree in Amazonia to have been carbon-dated. The one individual concerned was only 2.25m (7¼ft) in diameter, but was found to be 500 years old. It now looks likely that far more ancient Brazil nut trees exist.

All four species referred to above are tall, elegant trees, which produce a dome of lush foliage, emerging from the canopy at some 30–50m (100–165ft) from the ground. But they are not giants like the colossal kauris of New Zealand or the redwoods of North America. Their relatively slender trunks, which measure, on average, only 1–4m (3¼–13ft) in diameter, give no real indication that they are particularly old, although the trunks of all four species are supported by buttresses to varying degrees. Who knows how many other tree species that live to 1,000 years old the Amazon may contain?

A new threat to Amazonia's ancient trees

We now know that some of Amazonia's grand old trees have survived periods of environmental disruption such as droughts and possibly widespread fires, which are linked to climatic disturbances caused by El Niño, the warming of the eastern tropical Pacific Ocean. Climatological research has shown that devastating El Niño events occurred in the Amazon 1,500, 1,000, 700 and 450 years ago. Droughts of less severity currently arise every five to seven years in northern regions of the Amazon and are also linked to El Niño events.

In just the last seven years, however, two severe and highly unusual droughts have occurred in the Amazon region, which scientists fear are linked to man-made global warming. The drought of 2005 was followed by another, just five years later in 2010, which was even more intense, causing trees in the Amazon to produce more carbon dioxide than they absorbed.

Dr Simon Lewis of Leeds University, the lead author of a study into these events, said: 'If greenhouse gas emissions contribute to Amazon droughts that in turn cause forests to release carbon, this feedback loop would be extremely concerning … Two unusual and extreme droughts occurring within a decade may largely offset the carbon absorbed by intact Amazon forests during that time. If events like this happen more often, the Amazon rainforest would reach a point where it shifts from being a valuable carbon sink slowing climate change to a major source of greenhouse gases that could speed it up. Having two events of this magnitude in such close succession is extremely unusual, but it is unfortunately consistent with the climate models that project a grim future for Amazonia.'

Giant Amazon storm

As well as the serious drought, a devastating giant storm also hit the central Amazon rainforest in 2005, destroying an estimated half a billion trees. This estimate was made by scientists using satellite imagery that recorded changes in the reflectivity of the rainforest: the newly opened canopy has a changed reflectivity for only a few months before the forests start to regrow. For three days in January 2005, a storm measuring 1,000km (620 miles) long and 200km (125 miles) wide crossed the whole Amazon basin from south-west to north-east. Wind speeds of up to 145km/hour (90 mi/hour) were recorded and millions of trees were uprooted or snapped in half as the storm raged.

Uakari monkeys have specialized jaws which enable them to penetrate the hard surfaces of unripe fruits and eat nuts – such as Brazil nuts – that many other primates would not be able to consume.

YEW
The guardian of time

BOTANICAL NAME
Taxus baccata

DISTRIBUTION
Europe, North Africa and
west Asia.

**OLDEST KNOWN LIVING
SPECIMEN**
The Fortingall Yew in Perthshire,
Scotland: at least 2,000 years old,
possibly 5,000 years old.

RELIGIOUS SIGNIFICANCE
Held sacred by the early Indo-
European peoples, such as Celtic
and Nordic tribes.

MYTHICAL ASSOCIATIONS
Believed by ancient peoples to
be immortal and a symbol of
everlasting life.

CONSERVATION STATUS
Classified on the IUCN Red List of
Threatened Species in 2006 as of
'least concern'.

There is something awe-inspiring and magical about an ancient yew. With its massive trunk and evergreen crown it must have appeared immortal to our ancestors, standing virtually unchanged for centuries – a silent witness to the passage of time. In the deepest, darkest months of winter, when the forests were at their coldest and most forbidding, the yew must have given hope to early man, not only by remaining resolutely green in the face of a diminishing sun, but by often becoming ablaze with flame-red berries and filled with the excited chatter of birds – an island of life and colour at the bleakest time of the year. No wonder the yew became so venerated, and perhaps no other tree is so deeply interwoven with the ancient history of Indo-European people, or holds the same fascination and sense of mystery.

In evolutionary terms, the yew is truly ancient: yew-like fossils have been found in rocks that are over 200 million years old, pre-dating the dinosaurs. With the development of carbon-dating techniques, palaeontologists have been able to date fossils with increasing accuracy, and fossilized remains of *Taxus baccata*, which are indistinguishable from the modern tree, tell us that the yew existed around 15 million years ago, flourishing in forests during the upper Miocene Epoch. In addition, the discovery of yew pollen preserved in some of Europe's peat bogs has shown that yews were once much more numerous and widespread than they are today, at times forming a major constituent of European woodlands as far back as the Cromerian Interglacial Stage, which occurred between 750,000 and 450,000 years ago.

There are believed to be at least seven species of yew growing in the temperate forests of Asia, Asia Minor, India, Europe, North Africa and North America, but because of their similarity, some scientists feel that these may simply represent a series of variations or subspecies of *Taxus baccata*, the first yew ever to be scientifically described.

The immortal tree

The common yew (*Taxus baccata*) can be found growing wild throughout most of Europe, extending from Scandinavia and Estonia in the north as far south as the mountains of North Africa, and from Ireland in the west to the Russian Caucasus in the east. Yews grow from sea level in Britain and north-western Europe to altitudes of up to 3,350m (11,000ft) in the Himalayas. Common yews may be a major component of mixed woodlands,

The Tree of Life

The Tree of Life is a common theme among the ancient cultures of the world – it stands at the centre of paradise in Judaic, Christian and Islamic mythology, and at the centre of the world in Hindu lore. It is also key to many shamanistic traditions across Europe and Asia. Although it is impossible to know which species these trees might really have been, since the origins of the Tree of Life pre-date written texts, late Stone Age and Bronze Age artistic representations of yew-like symbols have been found in Spain, Greece, Turkey, North Africa, Siberia and many other locations. The yew's extraordinary ability to renew itself from decay and remain vigorous in the harshest of climates, and the symbolism of its blood-coloured fruit and blood-like exudates, must have been awe-inspiring to our ancestors. It is not hard to imagine how the yew could have found symbolic expression as the Tree of Life.

or occur in pure stands as groves or clusters, especially on steep valley sides, although few such woodlands now remain in the modern landscape. However, yew trees appear to thrive better than many others on steep chalk slopes, and what is acknowledged to be one of the finest yew forests in Europe is found on the chalk downland of Kingley Vale in Sussex, England. Outside Europe, Georgia and north-eastern Turkey have some particularly fine stands of monumental yews.

Common yews are not famous for the great heights they reach, but for the enormously thick trunks that they form in old age. With their deep reddish- or purplish-brown bark, and trunks that are often deeply fissured and fluted, they can measure up to 16m (52ft) in girth, becoming hollow with age. Another distinctive feature is their majestic spreading crown of dark green foliage.

Yew wood is one of the strongest and most durable woods known. However, as it approaches old age (i.e. 800 years old or so), the tree begins a unique process of self-renewal. The interior of the trunk and main branches slowly begin to rot away, aided by the sulphur bracket fungus (*Laetiporus sulphureus*), and after centuries this might leave little more than a frail, hollow shell. Such hollows can be as much as 3m (10ft) across. Some of these have been put to ingenious uses – in the nineteenth century, the Crowhurst Yew in southern England (over 4,000 years old) was fitted out as a room with tables and chairs, and on one side a doorway was cut.

Although the tree becomes hollow, the yew's life is by no means at an end then: this characteristic is part of the yew tree's strategy for survival, enabling it to renew itself, over many hundreds of years, from the inside out. Whilst, on the outside, new wood will begin to grow over and encase the old shell, producing layers of different textures and colours with enormous tensile strength, a branch, or more than one, may grow down from the tree to embed itself in the soil in the middle of the hollow trunk, forming an interior root. In time, this will become an interior stem and, finally, a new trunk.

Another way for the yew to extend its lifespan is by branch layering: a branch or branches dip down and slowly grow towards the ground outside the tree. Roots develop and new trees will grow up from these points, eventually forming a circular grove. Left undisturbed, this process can continue indefinitely, so that further groves are formed. Sadly, no fully established examples of yew groves exist today. Most of the trees old enough to re-establish themselves in this way are situated in churchyards, where it has often been deemed necessary to cut off branches growing near the ground.

ABOVE
If left undisturbed, the lower branches of a yew will layer naturally when they touch the ground.

OPPOSITE
The snake-like roots of an ancient yew in the grounds of Waverley Abbey in Surrey.

OVERLEAF
A rare pure yew stand in Dorset, south-west England.

The astonishing longevity of yews and their extraordinary ability to renew themselves from a state of great decay has set them apart from most other European trees and given rise to the concept of their immortality. As the late distinguished dendrologist Alan Mitchell said, 'We've now more or less agreed that these trees can be more than 4,000 years old. In fact, there appears to be no theoretical end to this tree, no reason for it to die.'

Assessing age

The extremely slow growth rates of mature yew trees, and the fact that most ancient yews become hollow over time, makes assessing their age difficult. To make matters more complicated, growth in yew trees can be very uneven. Some yews apparently lie dormant for a very long time. The Totteridge Yew in north London, for example, has maintained the same girth for nearly 320 years while giving every outward impression of good health, while others, such as the Crowhurst Yew in southern England, may be growing by only infinitesimally small amounts over extended periods. The conventional method of dating trees, by counting their growth rings or by carbon-dating the oldest timber, is not applicable to ancient yews as they not only develop hollow trunks in old age but have the very rare

The trunk of the magnificent yew at Crowhurst in Surrey could be 3,000 years old.

ABOVE LEFT
The hollow trunk of the Bettws Newydd Yew in Wales, which is 10m (30ft) in girth, with a new trunk developing inside.

ABOVE RIGHT
Many ancient trees have had to adapt to environmental challenges. The roots of these yews appear to flow over solid rock and fuse with their surroundings.

ability among trees to renew themselves even when of great age. In general, the life of a tree can be divided into three main stages: formative, when the trunk and crown are growing; mature, when the tree has reached its optimum size for the growing conditions; and senescence, when it has outgrown its ability to feed itself and starts to die back. The yew tree conforms to this model with a period of vigorous early growth followed by several hundred years of steady mature growth. However, for most trees, once they enter the period of senescence, the decline to death is inexorable. Yew trees, however, have the capacity to renew themselves by a process of vegetative regeneration, so a tree that may have stood quietly for hundreds or possibly thousands of years and increased in size only by tiny increments over centuries can suddenly resume vigorous growth.

The fact, then, that yews do not conform to the general growth pattern shown by most other trees, and that tree ring and carbon-dating methods are redundant on hollow trees, makes an accurate calculation of their age particularly challenging. The dating of ancient yews has had to rely mainly on the extrapolation of growth curves drawn from careful studies of trees whose planting dates are known, and measurements of annual growth rings taken from exposed areas of trunk or branches, or from fallen pieces of ancient wood. This data is then carefully interpreted, taking into account local conditions such as climate, soil type and exposure to light (shaded or not). Even so, different researchers using similar data have often come up with widely varying estimates of age. Dendrochronologists John Tabbush and Paul White arrived at a formula for calculating the age of churchyard yews from observations of growth rates, which suggests that a tree of 7m (23ft) in girth would be about 1,580 years old. However, yews do not conform to the same growth patterns as other trees such as oak and beech, which are familiar to foresters. Recent research by the Ancient Yew Group (AYG) in the UK suggests that a yew tree of 7m (23ft) or more in girth should be considered to be ancient and at least 800 years old, but beyond this, estimates of age are very difficult to substantiate. This is partly because yews have a virtually unique way of growing, surviving and regenerating, including their ability to 'return to formative' (i.e. vigorous) rates of growth at almost any stage in their very long lives. In addition, yew trees show vast differences both in their response to a range of locations and conditions, and also in the way that different individual trees grow. Even yews planted at the same time and in very similar conditions can produce a remarkable range of individuals. At Monnington Walk in Herefordshire, for example, 42 yews were planted in 1628 but by 2003, the trees varied in girth from 1.47–4.42m (4ft 11in–14ft 9in).

Knowing what we do about the ability of yews to lie dormant for hundreds of years and the extremely slow growth rates of ancient trees, one can only speculate on the exact age of the yew at Fortingall in Scotland, whose trunk has now split, but which was measured in the late eighteenth century at about 16m (52ft) in girth. An estimate of 2,000 years would not be unreasonable, but it could be up to 5,000 years old in the opinion of some experts.

The pegs mark out the full extent of the trunk of the Fortingall Yew before it split into several sections. It is possibly the oldest tree in Europe, with an estimated age of between 2,000 and 5000 years old.

There is a Yew-tree, pride of Lorton Vale,
Which to this day stands single in the midst
Of its own darkness, as it stood of yore:
Not loth to furnish weapons for the bands
Of Umfraville or Percy ere they marched
To Scotland's heaths; or those that crossed the sea
And drew their sounding bows at Azincourt,
Perhaps at earlier Crécy, or Poitiers.
Of vast circumference and gloom profound
This solitary Tree! a living thing
Produced too slowly ever to decay;
Of form and aspect too magnificent
To be destroyed …

WILLIAM WORDSWORTH (1770–1850),
'THE PRIDE OF LORTON VALE'

Distribution

The United Kingdom is believed to hold around 90 per cent of all the remaining ancient yews in Europe. The AYG's records show that there are at least 318 ancient yew trees in the UK – that is trees with a girth of at least 7m (23ft), indicating an age of 800 years or older. However, the distribution of *Taxus baccata* spreads into Asia also, and many of the most interesting finds, as well as much of the most exciting recent research, are coming now from the Russian Caucasus and northern Turkey. Here, a number of stands of 'monumental yews', real giants of the yew kingdom, are to be found growing wild in broadleaf forests. Records from a study of one such fallen yew near Khosta showed that it had just over 1,000 tree rings in a trunk that measured a mere 50cm (20in) in radius. This has given rise to the calculation that yew trees growing in the Caucasus region of south-western Russia that are over 2m (6½ft) in diameter are likely to be over 3,000 years old. In the Batzvara Nature Reserve in the Georgian Caucasus, a tree known as the Patriarch Tree (or 2,000-Year-Old Tree), which has a diameter of just 1.5m (5ft), was recently shown, by researcher Karlo Amirgulashvili using dendrochronology, to be about 1,530 years old.

The yew cult

No one knows who first venerated the yew, but it appears to have been central to the ancient animistic religions of Europe and western Asia, which revered the fertility of nature and which honoured and celebrated its renewal each year. To adherents of these religions, evergreen trees were associated with immortality. The ancient celebration that marks the winter solstice is a festival that appears to have been held since the dawn of human history. A mass of archaeological and petroglyphic evidence suggests that a European yew cult, involving the worship of the tree's scarlet fruits, its evergreen leaves and the golden pollen cloud of the male tree, is one of the oldest religious traditions known, and that it was from these that the ancient midwinter celebrations and the sophisticated beliefs represented by the Norse myths developed. The tree played a central part in the Nordic beliefs that held sway in the northern forests of Europe and which were marked by the worship of gods such as Odin and Ullr, the Norse god of archers, who was strongly connected to the yew. These in turn gave rise to belief in concepts such as Yggdrasil, a tree at the centre of the Earth with roots to the underworld, the land of the giants and the land of the gods. Later peoples, too, are known to have held strong beliefs associated with the yew – the Romans believed that it gave the souls of the dead safe passage to the afterlife, while the Saxons planted thousands of yew trees in Britain to mark the interment of their dead. Although it is difficult to determine the actual development of the Asiatic–European yew cult, it is

OPPOSITE
The Ankerwycke Yew by the Thames at Runnymede is believed to have been the tree under which the Magna Carta was signed in 1215.

likely that both people and religious ideas spread west across Europe, eventually
reaching Britain in 4000 BC. The Celts, who reached their maximum range in the
third century AD, are often associated with veneration of the oak, but yew trees
were certainly sacred to them and were planted on their holy sites. Many Celtic
tribes are known to have taken their names from the yew, such as the Iverni of
southern Ireland. The etymology of the word 'yew' is fascinating: despite its many
spellings in a range of ancient and modern languages across Europe, the sound
remains virtually the same – *yr* in old Norse, *yewar* in Celtic, *iva* in Middle Latin
and *iubhar* in Gaelic.

Sanctuary and catastrophe

Today, very few ancient yew trees are to be found in the wild in Europe. It is only
in parts of Asia, such as Georgia and northern Turkey, that ancient common yews
can still be seen gracing the hillsides alongside other woodland trees. Why is it that
the UK holds such a high proportion of Europe's remaining ancient yews? And why
are they so rare throughout the rest of Europe? The answers to these questions
are largely to be found under the headings of 'War' and 'Religion'. Yew trees were
a typical component of the wildwoods that stretched right across Europe during
each of the interglacial periods for hundreds of thousands of years. We are in an
interglacial period in the present era, so why are wild yew trees so rare? The answer
is that their destruction has been a catastrophic by-product of war. For thousands
of years, yew wood was utilized as the finest material for making longbows, which
were used for hunting. However, it was the medieval decree of King Edward I that
was to signal the beginning of the mass destruction of yew trees across Europe.
Edward decreed that every man in the British Isles should possess a yew bow
and arrows, but by the time Edward II was on the throne, in the early 1300s,
demand had already outstripped local supply and yew wood was being imported
from Ireland and Spain. Soon these countries ran out of yew trees too, and an
international trade developed, encouraged by the discovery that the Continental
yews, which grew at higher altitudes, made finer weapons. The yew bow became
the main weapon of war for about 400 years and the demand was colossal. Yew
timber was imported into Britain from Germany, Austria, Scandinavia, Spain
and many other European locations. The money earned made countries and
principalities hugely wealthy, but led to the destruction of millions of yew trees.
Records exist that support the estimate that in an 80-year period in just one area
of southern Germany and Austria alone, 1,600,000 yew staves were exported.
Surmising that this level of export was maintained across Europe for hundreds of
years, we can get some idea of the extraordinary magnitude of the destruction.
There seem to be two reasons why most of Europe's remaining ancient yews are to
be found in the UK. Firstly, British yews, it appears, were not as good for making

longbows as those from Continental Europe. The second reason is related to their location (at least the location of a great many of them) within the sanctuary of churchyards. There is evidence to support the fact that people avoided felling trees on consecrated ground and other yews that were considered sacred. It is curious that today, despite the fact that the UK is the home of most ancient European yews, it is also the country with the least protection afforded to these magnificent trees. Countries such as Germany and Austria have strict laws to protect yew trees, as does Georgia, whose laws to protect their monumental yews have already been in existence for nearly 100 years.

OAK
Spirit of the wildwood

BOTANICAL NAME

Quercus robur (the common, English or pedunculate oak)

Quercus petraea (sessile or durmast oak)

DISTRIBUTION

Across Europe, from Ireland in the west to Asia Minor in the east, and south to the Mediterranean coast of western North Africa. *Quercus robur* and *Q. petraea* are just two of over 600 species of oak that occur right across the northern hemisphere from Asia to North America, with the area of highest species diversity being Mexico.

OLDEST KNOWN LIVING SPECIMEN

Quercus robur: The oldest living specimen is believed to be the Kongeegen or King's Oak growing in the forest at Jaegerspris Nordskov in Denmark. It is currently 10.38m (34ft) in girth, but was measured at over 14m (46ft) in 1976, before part of the trunk broke off. The largest-trunked oak is the great Rumskalla or Kvill Eken in Sweden, which is currently 14.75m (46ft) in girth.

Quercus petraea: The largest
and possibly oldest sessile oak is
thought to be either the Pontfadog
Oak in Wales, which has a girth
of 13.38m (44ft), or the Marton
Oak in Cheshire, England, which
is 13.4m (44ft) in girth.

RELIGIOUS SIGNIFICANCE
Sacred to the ancient Norse,
Germanic and Celtic peoples, and
to the Greeks and Romans; some
individual trees have become
shrines.

MYTHICAL ASSOCIATIONS
Associated with the gods of
thunder and lightning among
ancient European peoples, and
with fertility; individual trees have
also become associated with
figures of legend such as Robin
Hood.

CONSERVATION STATUS
Q. robur classified as 'of least
concern'; *Q. petraea* classified as
'vulnerable' on the IUCN Red List
of Threatened Species in 2001.

O f all the native trees of Europe, the mighty oak has held a special fascination since the earliest times. With its distinctive broad crown, supported by a massive trunk in old age, this handsome tree has become an enduring symbol of strength, protection, durability, courage and truth.

Tree of strength

When the Swedish botanist Carolus Linnaeus (1707–78) used the term *robur* (from the Latin word for strength) to describe the common oak (**Quercus robur**), he was referring to two features that set it apart from many other trees: the robustness of the living tree and the great strength of its timber.

Oak timber is indeed synonymous with strength and durability. For thousands of years it has been used for construction purposes wherever permanence is required. Tree-ring evidence has proved that oak wood was being used in Germany some 9,000 years ago, and in Ireland 7,200 years ago. In Scandinavia, archaeologists have found that early Bronze Age coffins were hollowed out of oak trunks (or made use of naturally hollow ones), in order to give safe passage to the dead during their long journey to the next world. In Britain, King Arthur's Round Table was reputedly made from an enormous piece of oak, and the oak coffin (made from a hollowed-out tree) that rests in Somerset's Glastonbury Abbey is said to contain his remains.

Both the common and the sessile oak are very hardy and have co-evolved to be able to withstand attacks by pests and diseases, as well as exposure to extremes of temperature and drought. Even during the longest and most severe droughts, oaks seem to show few signs of suffering. This is true both of those that commonly grow in clay soils, which hold water well, and those found in drier, sandy regions. The vast edifice of trunk and crown is anchored to the ground by a network of tenacious roots. For the first few years of its life, the oak sends a large tap root into the soil, but other lateral roots soon develop into buttress roots, which stabilize the tree as well as drawing up water (around 90 litres/20 gallons a day).

Ageing ancient oak trees

While it is impossible to state with certainty which tree is the oldest oak in Europe, we can say that there are a number of great trees dotted across the continent, some of which have probably lived for more than 1,000 years.

There is much debate about just how old the most ancient oaks of Europe really are. The noted British dendrologist and co-founder of the Tree Register of the British Isles, Alan Mitchell (1922–95), felt that claims about the great ages of some oaks were often misguided. By plotting girth against age, he showed that in

their early years oaks actually grow quite fast, on average about 2.5cm (1in) per year, and that maturity is reached by about the age of 250 years, after which time the tree will slowly begin to die. 'The only open question', he wrote, 'is how much and for how long an oak over 25ft [7.6m] round can decrease in vigour, and so how much older than, say, 250 years it can be … to be 1,000 years old, it should be around 40ft [12m] round.'

The dating technique refined by dendrologist John White disagrees with the assumption that the trunk of an oak (and other ancient trees) will grow fairly constantly at about 2.5cm (1in.) per annum, and showed many ancient trees to be twice as old as previously thought. White's method is based on measurements of a tree's girth, and comparison of this data with other trees of the same species, size and, wherever possible, known planting dates on comparable sites. It also recognizes that trees grow at different rates during the different phases of their lives: formative, middle and old age.

The life of an oak is perfectly summed up by this anonymous quote: 'An oak tree grows for 300 years, rests for 300 years and then spends 300 years gracefully expiring.' Traditionally it has been considered that the biggest oaks in terms of girth are the oldest oaks. While this may be true, research has shown that trees growing in challenging environments, such as those that are waterlogged, those growing at high altitudes or subject to severe cold, have much smaller trunk sizes relative to their age. It is possible that in the future the oldest oak in Europe may

PREVIOUS PAGES
Oak trees have always been synonymous with strength and durability.

OPPOSITE
A mature oak in bluebell woodland.

BELOW
King Offa's Oak at Windsor in the third and final stage of its life – a collapsing giant over 1,000 years old.

Oak leaves and bark provide food or habitat for more insect species than any other European tree: at least 280 insect species are associated with oaks.

have only a modest girth compared to those colossal oaks that are considered ancient today. Many of the largest-trunked trees in the UK have been pollarded in the past, or have undergone a natural process similar to that of pollarding.

From medieval times until about 1800, pollarding was standard practice in many woodlands: it involved cutting off the trunk about 2.4m (8ft) up when the tree had reached a suitable height and at intervals thereafter, so that successive crops of smallwood (wood of a smaller diameter than the trunk, and useful for a variety of purposes) could be harvested later. The tree would re-sprout rapidly, and within a few years put on a much greater volume of foliage – often on about six spreading branches – than would a 'maiden', or uncut, tree. While a maiden tree depends on its original trunk, and dies when this does, a pollarded tree can continue to put out new shoots into old age, long after the original trunk has become hollow. In the UK, the discontinuation of pollarding may well be catastrophic for some of the most ancient oaks.

Ageing oaks is a very complicated business and there are a number of differing views on the subject. Guidelines recently produced for the Ancient Tree Hunt, for example, drawn from current research, stipulate that a 400-year-old oak could measure between 3–8m (10–26¼ft) in girth at a height of 1.3m (4¹/₂ft) depending on a variety of factors such as tree form (whether a pollarded or coppiced tree, for example), historic management and location. There are a number of other influences that affect the growth of an oak, such as soil type, altitude and exposure, but their influence is much more difficult to quantify. Interestingly, managed pollards are frequently found to be much older than their girth size might otherwise suggest, wherever they are, while pollards growing in woodland and on poor soil can be twice the age of a maiden tree that has grown in the open.

Another potential complication is whether a tree is a single trunk or was once a twin stem, as in the case of the Queen Elizabeth I Oak at Cowdray Park in southern England. It, like many of the UK's oaks with a girth of over 10m (33ft), formerly had two distinct main stems. However, the tree is still likely to be 600–700 years old. A good indication that a tree may have had two stems is given by its overall 'footprint', which will be more oval than round. This is also the case for the Major Oak in Sherwood Forest, Nottinghamshire, which is now considered to be nearer to 600 years old rather than 1,000 years old, as had previously been thought.

The ages given in the section below are estimations that have been made by taking into account the current scientific understanding of the ages of Europe's great oaks. Much research is now suggesting that the ages of the UK's and Europe's oaks should be reduced from previous estimates. Some researchers in the Netherlands and Germany believe that very few oaks live to over 500–600 years old, with perhaps a few examples living beyond 850 years. It is generally agreed, though, that some trees, such as the King's Oak in Jaegerspris Nordskov in Denmark and the Pontfadog Oak in Pontfadog, Wales have the potential to be over 1,000 years old. Whether their real ages are 500, 600, 850 or even 1,000 years old, the oaks described in this chapter are immensely old organisms that we should celebrate and protect as best we can for forthcoming generations as reservoirs of biological continuity, gene banks and as part of our living and cultural heritage.

The great oaks of the United Kingdom

The UK is richer in ancient oak trees than almost any other European country. Indeed, the Royal Parks at Windsor and Richmond near London contain more oak veterans than some entire European countries. However, this is not to say that there are not some truly magnificent ancient oaks to be found across Europe, or that the oldest oak is British.

The fact that so many ancient oaks are to be found in the UK is attributed partly to the land-tenure system that has prevailed since 1066, the absence of any large land-based wars (unlike the Napoleonic wars, for example, which led to the felling of hundreds of thousands of trees in Continental Europe) and the discovery of vast deposits of coal, which reduced the demand for timber. According to the Ancient Tree Hunt – a project that has recorded over 100,000 ancient and notable trees throughout the UK – in 2012 the UK had at least 43 oaks that exceeded 10m (33ft) in girth, and nine which were larger than 12m (40ft). These comprised an almost equal number of common and sessile oaks.

One of the largest oaks in the British Isles (and possibly in Europe), measuring 13.16m (43ft) in girth, is at Bowthorpe, near Bourne, on the flat Lincolnshire fens. With a hollow inside that measures 2.7 x 1.8m (9 x 6ft), it has been described by tree enthusiast Thomas Pakenham as 'a cave with branches growing from the roof'. It was apparently hollow nearly 200 years ago, when it was described thus: 'Ever since the memory of older inhabitants or their ancestors [it has] been in the same state of decay. The inside of the body is hollow and the upper is used as a pigeon-house.' A floor was installed in 1768 and benches added around the inside, so that the squire of Bowthorpe Park could dine inside with 20 guests.

Estimates of its age vary widely from 500 to over 1,000 years old.

In Moccas Park in Herefordshire, the ancient pollarded oaks, fondly called the 'crusty old men of Moccas', were described in 1876 by the clergyman and diarist Francis Kilvert (1840–79) as 'grey, gnarled, low-browed, knock-kneed, bowed, bent, huge, strange, long-armed, deformed, hunch-backed, misshapen oak men'. A number of these trees are also believed to be approaching 1,000 years old, especially the hunched and squat Old Man of Moccas. This park is home to the extremely rare Moccas beetle (*Hypebaeus flavipes*), which needs the presence of oaks that are at least 600 years old, and flowering hawthorns, to complete its life cycle.

Probably the most famous ancient oak in the British Isles, however, is the Major Oak, which stands in Sherwood Forest and takes its name from the local antiquary Major Hayman Rooke. Although neither the biggest nor the oldest oak, local people feel that it is very special indeed. Possibly the result of pollarding, and with some of its widest branches supported by 3m (10ft) posts, it is a very grand old tree, measuring 3.37m (11ft) in diameter. Alan Mitchell believed it to be only 480 years old, and it may well be that this is close to its true age. It now appears that it grew for much of its life in the open, away from other competing woodland species, which may have allowed it to reach a larger girth in less time than would have been the case had it been in deep woodland. It was beneath – some people say inside – this tree that the legendary Robin Hood (*c*.1250–*c*.1350), defender of the poor, is said to have met with his 'merry men'. This is unlikely, however, as the Major Oak is now considered to be 500–700 years old by most oak experts.

The tree commonly known as William the Conqueror's Oak, meanwhile, is one of several hundred ancient pollarded oaks known affectionately by their traditional name of 'dodders', which still stand in the Great Park of Windsor Castle and date from the Middle Ages. Today it has a circumference of 8.2m (27ft) and an enormous hollow in its trunk, which is said to have been large enough, in 1829, for 20 people to stand in, or 12 to 'sit comfortably down to dinner'. A tree known as Herne the Hunter's Oak, also in Windsor Great Park and dating from the thirteenth century, was mourned by Queen Victoria when it was blown down in 1863. Herne the Hunter was an oak god of southern Britain, whose spirit, with horns like antlers, was said to haunt Windsor Forest.

Possibly the oldest oak tree in the park and in the UK is King Offa's Oak, which also stands in Windsor Great Park. It is a magnificent crumbling ruin of a tree with a massive hollow and

As when, upon a trancèd summer-night,
Those green-robed senators of mighty woods,
Tall oaks, branch-charmèd by the earnest stars,
Dream, and so dream all night without a stir.

JOHN KEATS (1795–1821), 'HYPERION'

Words of strength and truth

In many different
languages, the word for
'oak' sounds remarkably
similar. In Scottish
Gaelic, for example, the
oak is 'dharaich', while
in Manx it is 'daragh'. In
Old Irish it is 'darach',
in Welsh it is 'derwen'
and in Greek it is 'drys'
or 'dru'. The words
are all related, linked
by the 'd…r…' sound.
They appear to come
from the same root
and to be linked to the
ancient Indo-European
(Sanskrit) word base
'deru', which means
'oak' and 'tree' as well
as 'firm and steadfast'.

The English word
'tree' is related also
to this word 'deru'.
So indeed is the word
'Druid'; for Druids,
oaks were magical and
a source of wisdom.
'Deru' also gave rise to
the words 'trust', 'tryst',
'troth', 'betrothe',
'truce', 'trow', 'durable'
and 'endure'. We use
words that have their
roots in ancient proto-
languages, unwittingly
it seems, when there is
something profound –
such as trust, strength,
or endurance – to talk
about.

a colossal fallen branch stretching away from the trunk. The bark and exposed timber provide surfaces on which mosses and lichens now grow, adding to the combination of browns, russets and copper-greens that light up this very beautiful tree. Ted Green of the Ancient Tree Forum, who has spent years working among the ancient oaks at Windsor, refers to this tree as 'the mother of all British oaks' and believes it is probably 1,300 or maybe even 1,500 years old.

Other ancient oaks in Britain include the Marton Oak in Cheshire, still flourishing but with a gap (formerly containing a calf shed) of 2.4m (8ft) separating the two remaining fragments of trunk, and measuring some 13.4m (44ft) in girth; the Billy Wilkins Oak in Dorset, said to measure 12m (39½ft) around its trunk, which is covered with burrs; the Judge Wyndham Oak, also in Dorset, which is a fraction under 10m (just over 33ft) round; the Old Man of Calke in Derbyshire which is one centimetre over 10m round (àt 1.5m), and the giant sessile oak at Pontfadog in Wales, which has a knobbly circumference of 13.38m (44ft). This is possibly Europe's largest sessile oak.

Some giant British oaks were so remarkable while they were alive that they are still remembered long after their demise. The Cowthorpe Oak, for example, which stood in South Yorkshire, was recorded as being larger than any living sessile or common oak today. Langdale's *Topographical Dictionary of Yorkshire* (1822) records: 'This oak in Yorkshire attracted many visitors on account of its age, its girth and its history ... the circumference of which, close by the ground, is 60 feet.' Although the tree collapsed nearly 100 years ago, the local people decided to leave the fallen timber to weather gracefully and serve as a reminder to this once colossal tree. The nearby church contains many words written in appreciation of the tree, including: 'Still let this massy ruin, like the bones of some majestic hero be preserved unviolated and revered' (J. G. Strutt, *Sylva Britannica*, 1822).

Many other great oaks are remembered in place and pub names, such as the Damory Oak in Blandford Forum, Dorset. It was reported that after the great

fire of Blandford Forum in 1731, two families lived
inside the hollow of this giant. Recorded as 20.7m (68ft)
in circumference and with 'room for 20 men inside',
it was eventually chopped down for firewood in 1755,
which raised the sum of £14 (around £1,200 today). The
Damory Oak pub sign shows children playing around
this great tree.

Europe's most ancient oaks

Many of the oldest examples of particular species of trees live in stressed
conditions and/or at the very limit of their range. The largest baobab tree,
for example, is also almost the most southerly baobab in Africa, and the
bristlecone pines on north-facing slopes have been shown to be able to live for
2,000 years longer than those enjoying the longer, warmer growing seasons of the
south-facing slopes. With this in mind, it is not unreasonable to assume that a
large oak growing almost at its most northerly extreme, exposed to bitterly cold
conditions, could be extremely old.

  The tree believed to be the largest oak in Europe is the Kvill Eken or
Rumskulla Oak growing near the village of Vimmerby in Sweden. It has a huge
girth of 14m (46ft) when the tree's many burrs are included and is still living today,
with a maximum estimated age of over 1,000 years old. However, two great oaks in
Denmark may be even older. The largest is the Kongeegen, or King's Oak, which
has a diameter of 3.6m (12ft) and a girth of 14m (46ft) but is in an advanced state

BELOW
The Kongeegen (King's Oak)
in Denmark is believed to be the
oldest oak in Europe.

of decline with only sparse foliage on top of its vast trunk. It
stands in the forest of Jaegerspris Nordskoven and is estimated,
even by the more conservative of tree experts, to be between 1,000
and 1,400 years old, making it probably Europe's oldest living
oak. Another oak found in the far north is the Stelmuž Oak in
Lithuania, which was thought to be 1,500 years old but it is now
considered much more likely that it is less than 1,000 years old.

  Some truly fantastic oaks with fascinating histories can be
found in many other European countries, including France and
Germany. In France we find the Chêne de Tronjoly, said to be
nearly 1,000 years old, which stands on a farm in Brittany. It has
a magnificent spreading crown and a bole that has split into two
parts, and measures 3.9m (12¾ft) in diameter (or a combined
circumference of 12.6m (41¼ft). Possibly contemporaneous with
it, the exact age of the Allouville-Bellefosse Oak, near Yvetot, is
not known. However, it has been a place of devotion for about
300 years – its massive hollow trunk (which measures 3.8m/12½ft

across) having had a chapel and a hermit's refuge cut into it. Two other large pedunculate oaks are found close to the church in Saint-Vincent-de-Paul, one of which has a girth of 12.5m (41ft).

Possibly the oldest oak in Germany (still alive, though very decayed) is to be found in the village of Erie, near Raesfeld in Westphalia. It is known as the Feme Eiche, or Trial Oak, since public meetings and trials were at one time held beneath it. This oak's age has been put, by some, at 1,500 years old, but is more likely to be between 600 and 850 years old. Near the village of Ivenack, north of Berlin, however, a grove of majestic oaks still stands. The trunk of the largest tree ascends for 7.6m (25ft) before the first branch occurs, and measures 12.4m (40½ft) in girth at 1m (3¼ft) from the ground. A sign nearby claims that it is 1,200 years old. Experts now believe it to be closer to 800 years old, but what is not in doubt is that it is the largest oak in volume in Europe, dwarfing many other ancient oaks including the UK's colossal Fredville Oak in Kent.

The more ancient the oak, the more species of insects, fungi and lichens it can support.

Beetles help tell the history of the wildwood

Many tree-lovers have a romantic notion of a time when Britain and much of Europe was covered by a vast, almost continuous closed-canopy forest dominated by majestic oak trees. However, recent research suggests that the history of British forests is much more complex. 'The Holocene forest was probably patchier than we thought: open areas were of local significance and an important feature of the landscape' says Dr Nicki Whitehouse, a palaeoecologist at Queen's University Belfast, who examines fossils to reconstruct past ecosystems.

Together with Dr David Smith, a specialist in environmental archaeology at the University of Birmingham, Dr Whitehouse has been looking at ancient beetle remains in an attempt to get a better understanding of the past. Beetles are useful because their remains are quite distinct from one another and many species have associations with very specific habitats. Some beetles, such as dung beetles, are indicative of open areas because they require the dung of grazing animals to survive, whereas others are dependent on rotting wood found in dense, closed-canopy forest.

By studying beetle remains, they found that the insect fossils from between 9500 and 6000 BC were mostly from beetle species associated with open woodland and pasture. There is evidence to support the theory that at this time the presence of large ungulates such as aurochs, wild horses and tarpans led to a dynamic mosaic of forest and open areas. And it is possible that the over-predation of the large grazers by humans then led to a subsequent expansion of forest areas. This may be why, between 6000 and 4000 BC, the beetle fossils changed to those

species more associated with closed-canopy woodland. Perhaps this was the golden age of trees that is set so deeply in the psyche of modern people.

However, by 4000 BC, it is thought that a huge change started to take place as humans began to develop an agricultural way of life, particularly with regard to the keeping of livestock. Neolithic people and their grazing animals helped return the landscape to a mosaic of pasture and woodland again by using grazing regimes and a land-management system that is known as 'wood pasture'. These open and closed areas provided good grazing as well as timber and non-timber products. This was a bonus for oaks, which prefer to grow on the edge of dense forest or in the open: the openings would have allowed more light in and the grazing animals would also have restricted the competition of the shade-tolerant species in the understorey. Unfortunately, with the expansion of the human population in Europe, agricultural practices lead increasingly to forest reduction and serious fragmentation, a process that has continued to the present day.

Ancient oak mystery

The theory that the oak was a special tree to our ancestors, connected with the supernatural, was strengthened in Britain in 1998. On the north Norfolk coast an extraordinary, mysterious structure was revealed by the shifting sands: an enormous oak tree stuck into the ground, with the stumps of its roots pointing upwards, surrounded by an oval ring of 54 oak trunks. This unique find, which may be the remains of an early Bronze Age tree temple, has been carbon-dated at 4,000 years old, making it as old as Stonehenge.

Ancient beliefs

A patchwork of woodland and open areas, as well as dense forests dominated by oaks, once stretched across large areas of Western Europe, shaping the lives of prehistoric peoples. To Norse and Germanic peoples and to the Celts, the oak was a sacred tree, and it was among holy oak groves that they made contact with their powerful gods.

A connection between the oak and ancient European storm gods developed long ago. Oaks are in fact more likely to be struck by lightning than most other European woodland trees, because of their size and because their electrical resistance is low. Belief in such a connection appears to have been common to the Aryan peoples who came to inhabit much of Europe and parts of Asia before the birth of Christ. To these people, the mighty oak formed a channel through which the power of the sky gods could reach the mortals on Earth – visibly demonstrated when a tree was struck by lightning and caught fire.

The kindling of fire from an oak log on midsummer's eve was a Celtic practice associated with fertility and probably accompanied by human sacrifice. Oak was also traditionally used for the Yule log that was burnt at the winter solstice, in the hope of drawing back the sun to warm the Earth. (In Rome, the Vestal Virgins –

priestesses of Vesta, the Roman goddess of the hearth – also used oak wood for their perpetual fires.)

The oak tree occupied a central position in the religious practices of the Celtic priests, the Druids. Though other interpretations are possible, the name 'Druid' has been translated as 'oak wisdom' and is said to derive from the Greek and Sanskrit words for oak, *deru*. The Druids revered the tree, as they believed it embodied the strength, power and energy of their mighty god Esus, and ritual sacrifices in his honour were performed amid their sacred groves. Mistletoe, a semi-parasitic shrub that can cling to the oak's branches under the right conditions, was also regarded as sacred, since it was thought to be a guardian of the tree.

Germanic tribes dedicated the oak to Donar, while in Norse mythology, the oak was sacred to Thor, who drove his chariot across the heavens and controlled the weather. Both were gods of thunder, and if a tree was struck by lightning, pieces of the splintered wood were kept as protective charms. At the end of the first century AD the Roman historian Cornelius Tacitus (*c*.55–120) mentions oak groves in north-west Europe that were especially sacred to Thor, many of which were subsequently destroyed by Christian missionaries. Belief in this deity was so strong that 'Thor's day' – now Thursday – was dedicated to him right across the Germanic world and regarded as a holy day.

The oak was likewise revered by the Ancient Greeks and Romans. The tree became sacred to the Greek god Zeus, the supreme being associated with the sky and weather, and to the principal Roman god Jupiter – the oak's association with lightning strikes, which were the special weapons of both these deities, was particularly significant.

To the ancients, the oak tree's special presence and powers included those of an oracle. In Homer's *Iliad*, Odysseus travelled to the famous oak that grew at Dodona to find out from its 'lofty foliage' the plans of Zeus. And according to the Greek poet Hesiod's *Catalogues*, the priestesses, who took the form of doves and lived in the tree's hollow trunk, imparted 'all kinds of prophecy' to those who travelled there.

OPPOSITE
One of the theories suggested for this wood temple is 'excarnation', during which bodies of the dead may have been exposed on the central upturned oak trunk.

ABOVE
A carved representation of the 'Green Man' garlanded with oak leaves, inside Sutton Benger Church, Wiltshire, England.

SWEET CHESTNUT
Tree of protection

BOTANICAL NAME
Castanea sativa

DISTRIBUTION
Southern Europe, western Asia,
North Africa.

OLDEST KNOWN LIVING
SPECIMEN
The Tree of One Hundred
Horses, Sicily: recorded in 1770
to have a bole measuring 62m
(204ft) in girth. Today, the two
largest remaining pieces measure
6m (18ft) in diameter at 1m (3ft)
from the ground. Estimated age:
2,000–4,000 years.

MYTHICAL SIGNIFICANCE
The Tree of One Hundred Horses
is believed to have sheltered the
Queen of Aragon and her retinue
of 100 cavaliers from a rainstorm
in 1308.

CONSERVATION STATUS
Not classified on the IUCN Red
List of Threatened Species.

PREVIOUS PAGE
Part of an avenue of ancient
sweet chestnuts at Croft Castle,
Herefordshire, England.

BELOW
The Tree of One Hundred Horses
(*Castagno dei Cento Cavalli*) as
depicted in 1784.

In 1308 Giovanna, Queen of Aragon, was on her way to view Mount Etna, Sicily's famous volcano, when she was surprised by a sudden rainstorm. Luckily for her and her escort of 100 cavaliers, they found themselves in the vicinity of a most extraordinary tree – one that was already famous for its colossal proportions and was apparently old at the time of Plato, the Greek philosopher (*c.*428–348 BC), some 1,700 years previously. The tree was a sweet chestnut (*Castanea sativa*), and so huge was its canopy of leaves and branches that Queen Giovanna and her entire retinue – so the legend goes – were able to shelter beneath it. This incident gave rise to the name by which this tree (which still survives in part) is known today: *Castagno dei Cento Cavalli*, or Tree of One Hundred Horses.

The colossus of Sicily

Situated near the village of Sant'Alfio, on the eastern slopes of Mount Etna, at about 550m (1,800ft) above sea level, the Tree of One Hundred Horses is considered to be the largest tree – in stoutness at least – ever recorded. In 1770 its bole was found to be an astonishing 68m (204ft) in girth. Like Europe's most ancient limes, oaks and yews, this chestnut had also become hollow in extreme old age. In 1670 the hollow was apparently so large that flocks of sheep were penned inside it. Some time later, a local family was also reported to be living inside the massive tree. Although by this time the chestnut had the appearance of a group

of trees growing together, excavations carried out over 200 years ago showed that all the parts were joined to a single root. By 1865, the tree had split into five distinct sections, of which today three separate pieces survive, 3.5–4.5m (12–15ft) apart. Though damaged, this once gargantuan chestnut – when in full leaf – still looks very much alive.

It would appear that the sweet chestnut's general decline (over the last few hundred years) has been provoked largely by the activities of people, within or around it. While the Tree of One Hundred Horses has recently been fenced to protect what remains, an engraving dated 1784 clearly shows a dwelling of some sort inside the tree, with pack animals tethered outside. One such hut was fitted with a kiln for drying the sweet chestnuts produced by the tree – an activity that cannot have been beneficial either to the roots or the living wood. Firewood was also apparently chopped from the tree.

The true age of the Tree of One Hundred Horses is difficult to establish, but it is generally considered to be 2,000–4,000 years old. That it should have survived the volcanic activity of the island for so long (it is only 8km [5 miles] from Mount Etna's crater) is indeed remarkable.

Early in the twentieth century, the slopes of Mount Etna were still graced by large numbers of sweet chestnuts, which formed 'dense forests', according to Mrs Grieve, whose famous herbal was published in 1931. Though none may be as old as the Tree of One Hundred Horses, other ancient sweet chestnuts survive nearby. The largest, with a diameter of 6.2m (20½ft), is located about 0.8km (½mile) away at Mascali, and is known as the Castagno della Nave or Ship Chestnut, because of its sheer size.

Herbal remedies

Medicine has long made use of extracts from the toothed, leathery leaves of the sweet chestnut, especially for coughs, catarrh and whooping cough, and also for diarrhoea. The famous English herbalist, physician and astrologer Nicholas Culpeper (1616–54) recommended taking chestnuts to thicken the blood. Throughout Europe the nuts themselves were traditionally carried as medicinal charms and were viewed as being therapeutic for many aches and pains, including rheumatism.

Ancient chestnuts of Europe

Possibly first domesticated in western Asia, sweet chestnuts are native to the deciduous woodlands of southern Europe (south of the Alps), and trees of great age and size, with girths of around 12m (39½ft), are to be found across the continent.

On the Italian mainland there are a number of enormous ancient chestnut trees. The one considered to be the largest complete tree in Italy today – in terms of its overall dimensions – is growing at Il Monte, near the village of Grisolia in northern Calabria. The survivor (along with two other smaller trees) of a grove of ancient chestnuts, it measures 4.3m (14¼ft) in diameter and is called, in the Calabrian dialect, the *Castagna del Salavrone* or Chestnut of the Green Lizard.

Possibly the largest tree in France – regarding the width of its bole at least – grows near the town of Pont l'Abbé in Brittany. This ancient tree, said to be 1,000 years old, measures just over 4.8m (16ft) in diameter at its base. Another vast French chestnut, standing on the southern shore of Lake Geneva near the town of Maxilly, close to the castle of Neuve Celle, is said to have sheltered a hermitage in 1408. The island of Corsica also has many ancient chestnuts, including the tree believed to be 1,000 years old still growing at Levie.

In Spain, the striking *Castaño Santo* or Holy Chestnut in the Sierra de las Nieves near Ronda in Andalucia, which has a girth of some 13m (42½ft) and an estimated age in excess of 800 years, has been declared a national monument and is a popular tourist attraction.

According to the Woodland Trust's Ancient Tree Hunt, completed in 2011, there are 19 enormous sweet chestnuts in the United Kingdom that are over 10m (33ft) in girth. Some of these can be discounted because they are multi-stemmed trees, but the Canford Chestnut, which stands in the grounds of Canford School in Dorset, the fourth largest chestnut in the UK, is a fraction over 13m (42½ft) around the trunk at breast height, while the largest surviving tree of what are known locally as the Three Sisters, in North Wales, is 12.7m (41½ft). However, the Tortworth Chestnut in Gloucestershire is probably the oldest in the UK today. Records show that this veteran was a prominent tree and boundary-marker as long ago as the twelfth century, and a legend suggests that it may have been planted around 800 AD during the reign of King Egbert. A plaque near the tree, dating back to 1800, reads:

> *May man still guard thy venerable form,*
> *From the rude blasts and tempestuous storm,*
> *Still mayest thou flourish through succeeding time,*
> *And last, long last the wonder of the clime.*

ABOVE
The Chestnut of the Green Lizard in Calabria is considered to be Italy's largest intact sweet chestnut today.

OPPOSITE
The largest of the 'Three Sisters' in North Wales with a girth of 12.7m (41½ft).

BELOW
The Tortworth Chestnut is believed to have been planted in 800AD. Written records of the tree go back as far as the twelfth century.

Uses of chestnut wood

In Britain today the sweet chestnut is grown commercially only for its timber. A vigorous, fast-growing tree, it responds well to coppicing, producing a good crop every 12–30 years.

In the past, sweet chestnuts were planted and coppiced in south-east England for charcoal manufacture, which was used extensively in metalworking. Kent and Sussex are the major areas for chestnut coppices today, and thousands of hectares are managed commercially.

Young sweet chestnut wood is hard, strong and rich in tannins, making it suitable for outdoor use. It is much valued for stakes, gateposts and paling fencing, which will last for 20 years or more, and for outdoor cladding (shingles) on buildings.

Sweet chestnut bark has been an important source of the vegetable tannin used for tanning leather in many European countries, including the UK, for many years. Italy is a major exporter.

In Italy, chestnut wood is also used to make barrels for ageing balsamic vinegar.

Today, though only a relic of its former self, with three huge branches resting on the ground, parts of the Tortworth Chestnut are still alive and flourishing.

The Romans are generally credited with introducing sweet chestnut trees to the British Isles, largely because of the finds of husks and nuts that have been made in a number of locations, including Hadrian's Wall in Northumberland. However, this may indicate only that chestnuts were one of the foodstuffs much favoured by the Romans, which were imported from Italy during the time of their occupation of Britain.

The sweet chestnut is well known for its vigorous growth and is therefore particularly suitable for growing as a coppiced tree. Its bark, purplish-grey in early life, becomes dark brown and deeply fissured with age, forming angled spirals of heavy ridges, or a network of ridges, when it is several hundred years old. Throughout its long life the glossy, dark green leaves of the tree are a characteristic feature, with their prominent parallel veins, each ending in a spiny 'tooth'. The fruits are also distinctive: sharp-spined, yellow-green husks that split open in the autumn, usually to reveal two shiny red-brown nuts.

Food for princes and lovers

'Delicacies for princes and a lusty and masculine food for rusticks, and able to make women well-complexioned.' This is how the British writer John Evelyn (1620–1706) described the noble fruit of the sweet chestnut. Evelyn lamented the fact that in England sweet chestnuts were chiefly fed to pigs, whereas they had been much loved by the Romans and were widely consumed across southern Europe and into Asia. In parts of Italy and on the island of Corsica, sweet chestnuts were a staple food for millennia, largely replacing cereals. They were in fact once used as a currency in Corsica and still form an important part of the local cuisine. They appear in a great variety of foods – from a type of polenta to local beer, soup and ice cream.

Sweet chestnuts are generally eaten roasted or boiled, but can also be processed to produce flour, bread, porridge, stuffing for poultry, fritters and delicacies such as the famous *marrons glacés* of France. They contain relatively low levels of protein and fat, but very large quantities of starch. For this reason, they were once widely used for whitening cloth.

Chestnuts remain an important part of people's diets across southern Europe, and it is still a popular weekend pastime in the autumn to collect them.

ABOVE
Unlike most other commercial nuts, which contain relatively large quantities of protein, sweet chestnuts consist of up to 70% starch, 5% fat and 4% protein.

OPPOSITE
Chestnut coppice is a familiar sight across parts of Europe. Trees are cut every few years to produce poles and timber for fencing and charcoal.

LIME
The dragon tree

BOTANICAL NAME
Tilia cordata (small-leaved lime)
Tilia platyphyllos (broad- or large-
leaved lime)

DISTRIBUTION
Both species spread across Europe.
Tilia cordata: from parts of the
British Isles and northern Spain in
the west towards Siberia and
Asia Minor in the east.
Tilia platyphyllos: a more limited
easterly spread, to Poland, western
Ukraine and western Turkey.

**OLDEST KNOWN LIVING
SPECIMEN**
Largest single trunk: The lime at
Staffelstein, Bavaria, Germany:
24m (79ft) in circumference,
estimated age: 1,240 years old
(but now a relic). Largest living
lime (*T. cordata*): the Heede
Riesenlinde in Lower Saxony: girth
17m (55¾ft) at 1.3m (4¹/₂ft),
height 26m (85¹/₄ft). Some limes
in Cumbria (UK) may be up to
1,600 years old.

RELIGIOUS SIGNIFICANCE
Believed to be connected with ancient fertility gods in eastern and northern Europe.

MYTHICAL ASSOCIATIONS
Regarded in ancient European folklore as female; connected in Teutonic myth with dragons.

CONSERVATION STATUS
Not classified on the IUCN Red List of Threatened Species.

Every other year in spring, the town of Schenklengsfeld in central Germany relives a ceremony that is centuries old. In the shade of the massive boughs of the ancient lime for which this town is justly famous, local people dressed in their regional costumes celebrate what has come to be known as the Lindenblütenfest – literally, the 'lime-blossom festival'. Among other festivities, men and women perform traditional dances beside the tree, which is one of Germany's celebrated Tanz Linde, or 'dance limes'. In former times, the dancing took place within the tree itself on a wooden dance floor that was constructed on the central branches.

Having long since rotted away, the interior of the enormous trunk, which has split into four separate parts, is completely hollow. Inside this hollow – some 6 sq. m (64 sq. ft) in size – a stone bears the inscription 'Gepflanzt im Jahre 760' (Planted in the Year AD 760). No one knows who positioned this stone, or whether the date is correct, but an age of around 1,240 years would not seem out of place, if one compares the size of this tree with other limes of known age. With a crown circumference of about 110m (360ft) and a trunk circumference of nearly 18m (59ft), this may be Germany's oldest lime. Other contenders for the title of oldest lime in Germany include the Kasberg lime in Bavaria and the Upstedt lime in Lower Saxony.

The tree is one of many enormous ancient German limes beneath whose spreading boughs people have been celebrating the arrival of spring and the fertility of nature since the distant past. In ancient European folklore the lime is represented as a female tree, and appears to have been regarded by early Germanic and Norse peoples as sacred to the ancient goddess of love and fertility, Freya (the counterpart of Venus), and to the goddess of married love and the hearth, Frigga (sometimes they are portrayed as one). In Estonia, according to lime expert Professor Donald Piggott, ancient lime trees were being worshipped by these peoples 'even after their late conversion to Christianity' and until recently, sacrifices and votive offerings were still made to them – sometimes attached to their branches by women hoping to be blessed with fertility.

Medieval poets came to use the lime as a symbol of romantic love, and the sweet-scented flowers that they described lovers lying upon seem likely to have included those of the lime tree, intoxicating those who smelt them with their heady scent. It is interesting to note that lime flowers – which have been used for centuries to make a medicinal tisane or tea – may, according to the famous herbal written by Mrs Grieve, 'produce symptoms of narcotic intoxication' if they are too old when used.

In France the lime was adopted as a symbol of love, friendship and gatherings. The lime in the village square at Lucheux, known as the Lovers' Tree, apparently sports a sign inviting newly wed couples to walk through its hollow trunk in order to bring good luck.

In Greek mythology, Cronos (son of Uranus and Gaia, Sky and Earth) is said to have changed himself into a stallion and sired the centaur Chiron, born to the sea nymph Philyra. So ashamed of her offspring was she that she beseeched the gods to turn her into a tree. She was duly turned into a lime tree – *phylra* in Greek.

Tree of justice, tree of dragons

By way of contrast with the lime's more romantic associations, it was also – certainly in Germany in the past – the tree beneath which justice was dispensed. The lime at Schenklengsfeld was one of these Gerichtslinden (or 'justice limes'), and was in use as such until the middle of the nineteenth century. It was here that many people were both sentenced and punished for their alleged crimes. Lime trees were also sometimes used as gallows.

This connection with the idea of justice perhaps explains why the planting of lime trees was adopted historically in Switzerland, Germany and France as a symbol of liberty and victory. A lime was planted in the city of Fribourg in 1476 to mark victory after the Battle of Morat, and many others were planted to mark the end of the Wars of Religion (1562–98). Many of the 60,000 trees planted in 1792 to mark the proclamation of the first Republic of France were also limes. In Sagy, Saône-et-Loire, a lime planted by the Duc de Sully was consecrated as a 'Tree of Liberty' in 1793.

In Scandinavia the lime was said to be one of the favourite haunts of elves and fairies, and it was considered unsafe to be near one of these trees after sunset. Ancient Scandinavian folklore also recounts that the mythical dragon Fafnir lived for 90 years in the ground, for 90 years in the 'desert' and 90 more in a lime tree, and there seems to be an interesting ancient connection between dragons and the lime. The legendary German hero Horny-Skinned Siegfried or Sigurd apparently acquired his name after he had slain Fafnir and bathed himself in its blood. It was after this feat that his skin became horny and invincible all over, except for one spot between his shoulders to which a lime leaf had stuck. In the German language, an old poetic term for dragon is *Lindwurm*, which translates as 'lime tree serpent' – perhaps the lime tree was once feared and revered as the haunt of mythical beasts.

OPPOSITE
The Hindenburg Lime is one of Germany's finest and oldest large-leaved limes.

OVERLEAF
The Tassilo Lime near the Bavarian village of Wessobrunn is believed to be around 1,200 years old.

Europe's ancient limes

Many of the ancient and enormous limes of Europe are broad- or large-leaved limes (*Tilia platyphyllos*). These, and the closely related small-leaved lime (*Tilia cordata*), belong to the genus Tilia; this comprises some 23 other species and 14 subspecies according to Professor Donald Piggott, though research carried out on species in China and USA may well alter the number of what are acknowledged to be distinct species and subspecies in the future. Of the four species native to Europe, the broad-leaved lime is the first to flower (in late June),

… Comes sudden on my heart, and I am glad,
As I myself were there! Nor in this bower,
This little lime-tree bower, have I not marked
Much that has soothed me. Pale beneath the blaze
Hung the transparent foliage; and I watched
Some broad and sunny leaf, and loved to see
The shadow of the leaf and stem above
Dappling its sunshine! …

SAMUEL TAYLOR COLERIDGE (1772–1834),
'THIS LIME-TREE BOWER MY PRISON'

Lime bast and the prehistoric people of Europe

Lime trees were once very important to the ancient peoples of Europe because the fibrous layer or bast, located just under the bark, provided the material from which rope and other essential items could be made. The 5,300-year-old Ice Man discovered in 1991 in the Austrian Alps had a knife sheath made of knotted lime-bast fibres, and dried lime bast inside his shoes to keep his feet warm.

Cordage has been made from lime bast in northern Europe from the Mesolithic period (9000–3000 BC) until the present day. It was traditionally made by stripping sections of bark from trees in midsummer, and submerging this in water to help separate the layers. The outer bark was peeled away to reveal the bast. This could be spun and twisted to make lightweight cords and ropes, stronger when wet than those made from the fibres of any other European tree.

generally producing three to five large pale yellow flowers hanging from a whitish-green bract. With a natural range that extends right across Europe from northern Spain and Sweden, east to the Crimea, the Caucasus and Asia Minor, broad-leaved limes have been widely planted in European parks and gardens, and also as street trees in towns, sometimes forming elegant avenues.

With an impressive crown that forms a towering dome of radiating branches in maturity, the large-leaved lime is regarded as a very shapely tree, capable of reaching giant size, considerable height and very great age. In Lithuania and Poland large, majestic old limes, whose branches may form a canopy over 30m (100ft) up from the ground, make up a large component of the ancient wild forests, such as the famous Bialowieza Forest. France is also noted for some remarkable giant limes, such as the Estry Lime in Calvados, Normandy (said to be over 1000 years old), but it is in Germany that many of the most outstanding ancient individuals are to be seen.

A huge 1,000-year-old tree, some 30m (100ft) tall and with a wide-spreading canopy, is growing in the Bavarian town of Hoffeld. Almost as tall is the magnificent tree known as the Hindenburg Lime (*Hindenburg-Linde*), which stands just a few yards from the Alpenstrasse, above the village of Ramsau in south-east Bavaria. This tree is about 26m (85ft) in height, has a trunk 11.5m (38ft) in circumference, a beautiful, broad-spreading crown, and is also believed to be about 1,000 years old.

This old coppiced lime in the Lake District in England is believed to be around 1,600 years old.

Coppiced limes are difficult to age, but this practice enables small-leaved limes to live beyond 1,000 years.

Another ancient Bavarian lime tree, the Tassilo-Linde, thought to be at least 1,200 years old, is to be found in the village of Wessobrunn. An enormous tree, its hollow trunk measures 13.3m (44ft) in circumference at breast height. In the eighth century it formed part of the wildwood or *Urwald* that covered the region, and appears already to have been a large, impressive individual at that time. It is recorded that beneath this tree, Duke Tassilo III lay down to sleep after hunting in the surrounding forest. As he slept, he dreamt that he saw three springs whose waters flowed together in the form of a cross, and that above this spot a Jacob's ladder appeared, with angels climbing up and down it. On waking from his dream, the duke asked his hunting guides to look for the springs he had dreamt of. A guide named Wezzo (after whom Wessobrunn is named) found the spot and it was here, in the year 753, that the duke decided to found a Benedictine monastery, which, with its baroque and rococo works of art, is well known today. The Tassilo-Linde is only a few minutes' walk from the monastery and has now become a place of pilgrimage in its own right.

Other impressive ancient limes in Germany with a trunk circumference of 16m (52ft) or more include the tree at Heede, and the trees at Kötzting and Kasberg, both in Bavaria. According to the German publication *Unsere Baumveteranen* (*Our Tree Veterans*), 20 trees are listed as having reached at least 1,000 years old. One of these is the lime at Upstedt, near Bockenem in Niedersachsen, said to have been planted in AD 850. The tree that is now possibly the widest of any species in Germany is a huge lime growing at Staffelstein in Bavaria. Some 25m (82ft) in height, its trunk is 24m (79ft) in circumference and 7m (23ft) in diameter – making it one of the broadest-trunked trees in Europe. Legend has it that this tree was

Sweet medicine
Limes produce a mass of sweet-smelling flowers in early summer. A herbal tea can be made from them, and they have also been used to flavour sweets and liqueurs. The famous English physician Nicholas Culpeper (1616–54) recorded that lime-flower tea was good for apoplexy, vertigo and palpitations of the heart, but nowadays it is said to be effective as a general tonic. Lime blossom is also used in some beauty preparations to help soothe the skin. Mixed with lavender flowers, it is sometimes used as a filling for herbal pillows to help induce sleep.

planted to celebrate the coronation of King Charlemagne in AD 800. While this cannot be verified, research on the Great Lime of Burghley in Lincolnshire in the UK has shown that the suggested planting date for the tree at Staffelstein may not be unreasonable: in 1986 the Burghley lime had a trunk that measured 2.3m (8ft) in diameter and was known to be 425 years old.

In England, the occurrence of large-leaved limes (which arrived from Europe with their small-leaved relatives about 8,000 years ago) is much more restricted than it is in Germany. However, some enormous specimens are still to be found. Probably the most famous is the striking tree growing at Pitchford Hall in Shropshire, which proudly supports a restored eighteenth-century tree house – replacing one from the seventeenth century – among its giant limbs. Measuring about 7m (23ft) in girth and with branches that are some 2.4m (8ft) in circumference, this tree certainly appears ancient.

The small-leaved lime is also to be seen in European parks and gardens. Confusingly, its attractive leaves are often similar in size to those of its large-leaved relative. This tree was once very important in lowland England and Europe. Discoveries of preserved pollen and fossilized bark-beetles that feed only on lime show that it played a major role in shaping Europe's native woods. Indeed, it dominated the original wildwood over a large area of the English lowlands and the central European plain, reaching a peak around 5,000 years ago.

Coppicing, pollarding and immortality

The enormous width of many lime trunks and, indeed, the very great ages that these trees can reach has been discovered to be largely due to the ancient practices of pollarding and coppicing. A pollarded tree is one whose trunk has been cut at around 2.5–5.5m (8–18ft): this leaves a permanent broad trunk and over a lengthy period a noticeably swollen 'pollard head' or 'boll', where new shoots spring up each year. A coppiced tree is cut near ground level, leaving a low base or 'stool'. Both methods stimulate the production of new shoots, which are also cut when they have reached the right size.

The practice of coppicing produced what was once thought to be the oldest lime in the world. A small-leaved lime growing at Westonbirt Arboretum in Gloucestershire was estimated to be over 1,000 years old because the enormous coppice stool measured 16m (52ft) across and had 80 individual trunks rising from it. However, recent research into the lime's response to coppicing has shown that after each 'harvest', the coppice stool puts on a spurt of lateral growth that can be equivalent to 50 years of growth rings in some cases. Therefore, large-diameter coppice stools are likely to be much

younger than previously supposed. There is, however, evidence to suggest that the ancient coppiced limes living at their northerly limit on steep slopes in the Lake District in the UK may be over 1,600 years old.

Today the existence of ancient coppiced or pollarded limes in woodland is considered to be a good indication that the woodland is very old – directly descended from the wildwood of old. The ancient wild limes in Britain's woodlands are not, however, the towering trees of majestic proportions still to be found in undisturbed woods elsewhere in Europe (such as France, Poland and Lithuania), and this has led to their ancient status often being overlooked. History shows us that lime trees have been important to people throughout Europe for thousands of years. It is interesting to reflect that ancient woodland-management techniques, performed in the right way and at the right time, actually prolong the life of the tree; indeed, they would seem to make it almost immortal.

OLIVE
Tree of peace

BOTANICAL NAME
Olea europaea

DISTRIBUTION
All countries bounding the
Mediterranean; also cultivated
in other warm temperate or
subtropical regions.

**OLDEST KNOWN LIVING
SPECIMEN**
Possibly the Ano Vouves tree,
which may be 4,000 years old
(on the Greek island of Crete) or
the Cormac's Tree on Sardinia,
estimated to be between 2,000
and 5,000 years old.

MYTHICAL ASSOCIATIONS
Sacred to the early peoples of the
Near East and to the Egyptians,
Greeks and Romans. Believed
by the Greeks to be a gift from
the goddess Athena, and by the
Romans to be linked with the
goddess Minerva.

CONSERVATION STATUS
Not classified on the IUCN Red
List of Threatened Species.

O f the world's most venerable and ancient trees, perhaps none is more closely associated with the history of humankind and the development of Western civilization than the olive. Sacred to the Greeks, Romans and Egyptians, and revered by the early Semitic peoples of the Bible lands, the olive tree – the source of food and valuable oil – has, for thousands of years, been central to the religion, cultural life, economy and cuisine of millions of people in the Mediterranean region. Its extraordinary ability to renew itself from destruction or decay by producing new shoots and roots greatly influenced people in ancient times to regard it as sacred, and to celebrate its significance in myth and legend.

To the Ancient Greeks, the olive was a gift from Athena, the goddess of wisdom and the daughter of Zeus, who struck the rock of the Acropolis with her spear and created the first olive tree. In so doing she won the gods' favour, and hence took control of the city of Athens (which was named in her honour) away from the powerful god Poseidon. Every year, the festival of Athena was celebrated as a public holiday, during which olive branches were carried to the Acropolis. At the Olympic Games, the Ancient Greek athletic festival held at Olympia, vases filled with sacred olive oil were given as prizes, while the victors wore olive wreaths.

To the Romans, the olive was sacred to Minerva, the goddess of health and wisdom, and it was she who taught the art of olive cultivation. In Egyptian mythology it was Isis, wife of Osiris, who held the secrets of the cultivation and use of olives. In Islam, the olive became the Tree of Blessing, giving to the world the light of Allah.

Although its botanical name (*Olea europaea*) suggests a European origin, six subspecies of olive, all genetically different, are spread over a wide area: from Madeira and the Canary Islands in the East, across the Mediterranean Basin, and from eastern and southern Africa, across Arabia to southern China. Fossilized leaves dating back to 37,000 BC have been found on the Aegean island of Santorini, and olive stones that are 20,000 years old have been discovered in Israel.

It is thought that the olive may have been domesticated in the eastern Mediterranean or the Nile Delta, but its immediate ancestry is uncertain. It seems likely, however, that careful tending and experimentation by generations of prehistoric people – who discovered that olive shoots could be grafted and replanted – refined and encouraged the tree's productivity. With careful pruning and the right environment (hot summers, but winters cold enough to set the fruit), the olive tree could be nurtured to yield superior fruit.

The harvesting of olives has been a way of life for people in Mediterranean countries for thousands of years.

A precious resource

In ancient times, the religious and ceremonial uses of olive oil were highly significant. In the scriptures and in classical writings, olive oil is referred to as an emblem of goodness and purity, and it may have been this oil that formed the base for the 'ointment of spikenard' used to anoint Jesus' feet before the Last Supper. In Biblical times, olive oil was also regarded as an emblem of sovereignty, and it played an important role in coronation ceremonies. When Saul, the first king of Israel, was crowned, olive oil was rubbed into his forehead. Olive oil was further used in the preparation of sacrificial offerings, in funeral rites, perfumes and cosmetics, and as an aid to healing. In Psalm 128, olive trees are a symbol of prosperity and plenty, and of divine blessing: 'Happy are those who obey the Lord, … your sons will be like olive trees around your table.'

According to experts on the plants used at that time, the general references to 'gardens' in the Bible are often references to olive orchards or groves. The wealthier the owner of such an orchard, the more likely he would be to grow other fruit trees there (such as figs, almonds and pistachios), but the tree that no one could do without was the olive. The major attraction of such gardens was – and still is – the provision of shade from the intense heat of the sun, a place to retire to during the day and, at the appropriate time of year, the supply of olives for food and oil.

The most famous garden of this kind is described in the New Testament – the Garden of Gethsemane. This was an orchard situated at the foot of the Mount of Olives, where oil presses where located. Before his betrayal and crucifixion, Jesus went to the Garden of Gethsemane with his disciples to pray: 'Jesus left the city and went, as he usually did, to the Mount of Olives' (Luke 22:39). It was there that

Olive trees growing on ancient terraces in the Bcharré Valley, Lebanon.

he was seized and subsequently nailed to the Cross, said to have been made in part from olive wood. Although little remains of the original Garden of Gethsemane today, some of the ancient olive trees growing there are said to have been planted at the time of Christ, making them about 2,000 years old.

It was largely the production of its precious oil that made the olive a crop of such fundamental importance to the lives and economies of the peoples of the Mediterranean and the Near East. Olives became the currency of the Mediterranean and a cultural inspiration for the great empires of Assyria and Egypt, and those of the Greeks, the Persians and the Romans. Some of the most beautiful artefacts left behind by these peoples, including frescoes and mosaics, depict aspects of olive cultivation.

Archaeological evidence and scientific studies suggest that the Minoans were cultivating olive trees on the island of Crete 5,200 years ago. Olives were certainly of major importance to the Phoenicians, a Semitic people whose civilization on the coastal plain of Syria flourished after 1800 BC. Becoming outstanding navigators, they established trading posts all over the eastern Mediterranean and beyond, and are thought to have taken olive cultivation to Provence (then known as Massilia) in southern France in 600 BC, grafting cuttings taken from olives in Asia Minor onto wild trees there. Archaeological excavations have shown that large olive plantations were in use at Aix-en-Provence and at other locations in southern France at that time. The Phoenicians also planted huge olive groves in North Africa, while Moorish travellers from this region were subsequently to take many olive trees to Spain.

By 1500 BC the Egyptians, who also revered the olive, had taken the tree from Syria to Egypt to cultivate it themselves. So important were olives to the Egyptians that golden carvings of them were sealed into pyramids with some of the mummified pharaohs.

Wherever the Greeks went, they took the olive with them. They took olive trees to Sicily, for example, between the tenth and eighth centuries BC, and by the sixth century BC they had felled most of their own native forests in order to grow them, building an entire export industry based on olive oil. Using the wealth derived from wine and oil, the Greeks built the great Sicilian city of Syracuse and took olives to the Italian mainland.

By 600 BC, the olive had also become an important crop for the Romans – so much so that they had a separate stock market and merchant navy for olive oil. It is said that they became such experts on the different kinds of olives they

ABOVE
It has been suggested that olives still growing in the Garden of Gethsemane in Israel could date back to the time of Christ.

OVERLEAF
Morning sunshine filters through the branches of a young olive tree in Greece.

grew that a popular amusement at banquets was the blindfolded identification of certain olives and their oil. The fruits themselves were used as snacks and appetizers (much as they are today), and in cooking. The Romans also planted large olive groves in North Africa and France. By the tenth century AD, such groves were to be found at the fringes of the entire Mediterranean, across southern Europe and in North Africa.

The beauty of the olive tree has been extolled in works of art for thousands of years. Images of the trees or fruit have been depicted in Minoan frescoes, on Grecian pottery jars, Roman silver vases and in countless friezes and carvings of the ancient world.

The immortal olive

With their lance-shaped, evergreen leaves – a deep grey-green above and silvery white on the underside – and gnarled grey trunks that develop in old age, olive trees form one of the most characteristic aspects of Mediterranean vegetation. Though they may reach about 15m (49ft) in height, olives are generally small trees, and in some areas (such as Provence, Greece and Cyprus) they are pollarded at 5–7m (16–23ft) to improve the crop and to make harvesting easier.

The olive matures very slowly and may need several decades to reach full maturity and productivity. Its crop is not said to diminish until an age of 150 years has been reached, but even long after this, it is still capable of bearing a good harvest. Pliny refers to an olive grove that was still producing fruit even though it was over 700 years old. In maturity, olive trees become grotesquely gnarled, in wonderful contrast to their light, silvery foliage. By about 200 years of age the olive appears truly ancient: its branches and trunk have become twisted and contorted, and shoots develop at its base, which will eventually grow up to form a new tree.

Some botanists believe that an individual olive trunk will not live for much longer than about 700 years, but the tree's massive root ball will continue to throw out new shoots for centuries. New roots are also formed when the old roots die.

This tendency, and the tree's ability to produce new shoots, or suckers, which will become a new tree even after the trunk has died or been felled, have given rise to the reputation of the olive as an immortal tree. With a similar capacity for regeneration as the yew, small-leaved lime and sweet chestnut, it certainly shares the distinction of being among Europe's oldest trees. Pliny the Elder (AD 23–79), the Roman naturalist and chronicler, recorded that the Athenians venerated one such tree, which they claimed was 1,600 years old. Even if it were true that the Roman emperor Titus Vespasian (AD 9–79) did – as was reported by contemporary scholars – cut down the olives growing in the Garden of Gethsemane in AD 70, it would appear that he did not actually kill them.

Just how long the olive can in fact live, and which tree is actually the oldest, is the subject of much debate. A number of trees are cited as being over 1,500 years old, including one on the island of Brioni in Croatia, calculated to be about 1,600 years old, an olive tree in Bar, Montenegro, which is claimed to be over 2,000 years old, and another in the Algarve of a similar age. On Crete there are many ancient olives and one of these, in the village of Ano Vouves, is claimed by some to be the oldest in the world. Tree-ring analysis has indicated that the tree is at least 2,000 years old, while studies carried out by the University of Crete have led to estimates of an age of some 4,000 years. On Sardinia, an olive known as the Cormac's Tree is believed to be more than 3,000 years old. Other individual ancient specimens

include those at Filitosa in Corsica (estimated to be 1,000 years old, and possibly as old as the megaliths that surround it) and at Roquebrune on the French Riviera (one is known as the 'King of Kings' and is reputed to be 2,000 years old). The truth is that the land around the Mediterranean is studded with ancient olives, some of which are likely to be over 2,000 years old, and since the majority haven't been examined scientifically, establishing the most ancient individual amongst these is an almost impossible task.

Cultivation

Needing very little water and able to survive on parched, dry soils, the tenacious olive can search out moisture at great depths, sending its roots down some 6m (20ft) in search of it. Olives are, however, very responsive to irrigation and fertilizer, and will produce a heavier and a more reliable crop if given this care. But to produce any useful quantity of fruit, the olive is dependent upon human hands in other ways, since the trees require grafting. Trees that grow up from seeds or suckers will produce only small, inferior fruit; they must be budded or grafted on to an established variety to do well. Cuttings are often grafted on to the stumps of

old trees. Today, several hundred named varieties – or cultivars – exist, but of these, **139** varieties account for **85** per cent of the olives grown as a commercial crop.

In early summer, olive trees produce a multitude of small, white, perfumed flowers, which appear in groups under the preceding year's leaves and are pollinated by wind. Strong winds, heavy rain and spring frosts, however, can kill the flowers, so the production of fruit is erratic: trees may produce a heavy crop one year and not even bloom the next. The familiar black or green olives that we buy are not produced by different trees: the olive's fruits are green at first but become a satiny dark blue or purplish blue-black as they ripen, bursting with yellow oil. In this mature state they cling to the tree for several weeks before falling to the ground. Olive-growing is a special art – continued by countless generations of traditional small-scale farmers – requiring patience and skill, and a special empathy with the trees. As one French grower from Provence put it: 'Olive trees respond to man, they interact … There is no more passionate tree anywhere, nothing that relates to man like an olive.'

An interesting belief arose, in parts of the Mediterranean, that the production of olive fruit was influenced by the moral standing of the picker. Thus, for a time

> *The murmur of an olive grove has something very intimate, immensely old. It is too beautiful for me to try to conceive of it or dare to paint it.*

VINCENT VAN GOGH (1853–90)

in Ancient Greece only virgins and young men sworn to chastity were allowed to harvest the trees. Until recently, in some parts of Italy, a common tradition also held that the olive crop was sensitive to virtue. If tended by young, innocent children, the olive yield would be prolific; a farmer who was unfaithful to his wife could expect his misdemeanours to be reflected in a poor harvest!

Olives have signified land, or rather rights to land, for thousands of years. Many peoples – such as the Palestinians – feel that their identity is intricately linked to their trees. But today in the Holy Land olive trees have become, sadly, objects of war rather than symbols of peace and trees are being destroyed, often as a first move, in battles over land.

The olive harvest

In the Mediterranean region the ancient olive harvest takes place during the autumn and winter months, varying from region to region according to the climate and the requirements of the grower. As a general rule, harvesting by hand is still the most common method because it allows the best fruits to be selected for eating as 'table olives' without damaging the trees.

In other places, the olives are left to fall to the ground naturally; another method, often employed in Italy and Spain, is to use a long pole to beat the trees, or a kind of long-toothed comb may be stroked through the foliage to loosen the fruit. In biblical times, olives were also gathered by shaking or beating the trees, but a few fruit would always be left on them, it was said, for the poor, strangers, orphans and widows to gather.

It takes about 5kg (11lb) of olives to make 1 litre (1¾ pints) of oil, most of which comes from the outer flesh of the olive. In the eastern Mediterranean, the simplest and most ancient means of pressing olives dates back over 6,000 years. The olives are first crushed in a mortar and the resulting paste transferred to an earthenware jar. Hot water is then poured over the paste while it is kneaded by hand. As olive oil is lighter than water, the oil released from the fruits floats to the surface, allowing it to be skimmed off.

People who live among olive trees talk of the air being purer because of them. When Jeanne Calment of Arles in France was asked, on her 121st birthday (shortly before her death in August 1997), how she had survived to be the world's oldest woman, she answered simply: 'Olive oil!'

OPPOSITE
A harvester knocks olives
from a tree onto nets spread
beneath them.

WELWITSCHIA
Dwarf tree of the Namib desert

BOTANICAL NAME

Welwitschia mirabilis

DISTRIBUTION

The northern gravel plains of the
Namib Desert, from the Kuiseb
River to southern Angola.

OLDEST KNOWN LIVING
SPECIMEN

Carbon-dating of the largest
Namibian trees indicates that they
are more than 2,000 years old.

CONSERVATION STATUS

Not classified on the IUCN Red
List of Threatened Species.

Of all the strange and wonderful ancient trees around the world, the welwitschia is perhaps the species that looks most like an extra-terrestrial form of life. Half-buried in the sands of the lunar landscape of the Namib Desert, it is unlike any other tree. The first European to discover it (in 1859), after whom it is named, was the Austrian-born doctor and botanist Friedrich Welwitsch (1807–72). So bizarre did the plant seem, he was afraid to reach out and touch it, fearing that it was simply a mirage.

Welwitschia mirabilis is now known to exist only on the gravel plains of the northern Namib Desert, from the Kuiseb River to southern Angola. In some areas, such as Swakopmund, welwitschias exist in large numbers and form the dominant vegetation. The ancestry of the welwitschia is thought to be extremely ancient and it is regarded as a 'living fossil' – a link with the prehistoric flora of the super-continent Gondwana, which existed millions of years ago. The form and proportions of the welwitschia are so unusual that there is nothing else comparable in the plant kingdom. It is so unlike any other plant that it is a unique species, occupying its own genus.

The name given to the tree by the Topnaar, who live in the western central Namib Desert, is *Otji-tumbo* or Mr Big. The 'trunk' of the welwitschia takes the form of an inverted cone, like a giant parsnip, and is almost entirely buried under the sand. It can reach a girth of 1.2m (4ft) or more and rarely rises more than 1m (3ft) above the ground, but tapers into a tap root that penetrates the desert floor by some 3m (10ft). Although primarily a water-storage organ, the trunk is reported to be as hard as the hardest wood and covered in a corrugated, cork-like bark.

PREVIOUS PAGE
The extraordinary welwitschia growing in the desert near Swakopmund in Namibia.

BELOW
The Welwitschia has adapted to the harsh environment of the Namib Desert, which receives less than 3cm (1 ¼in) of rain each year.

From the subterranean trunk, a crown of dishevelled foliage spreads out across the arid desert surface. This typically appears as a mound of vegetation torn to tatters by the desert wind. Strangely, the adult plant bears just a single pair of leathery leaves, which emerge from deep grooves on opposite sides of the broad, squat 'trunk', with a pronounced crater in the centre. The leaves, which are greenish-brown in colour, can grow to a staggering 1.8m (6ft) in length in old trees, and are the only ones ever produced during its entire lifetime – which may extend to thousands of years. As the leaves develop, they become broad, leathery and heavily ribbed; over time they are torn into narrow ribbons by the fierce desert winds. These ribbons become twisted, bent and entangled and lie in tattered heaps on either side of the crown.

Everything about the welwitschia is curious, including its flowering habit. Trees are either male or female – the male trees have erect scarlet cones that rise about 30cm (12in) above the trunk, and 'flowers' that sprout from the scales of the cones. The pollen is conveyed to the reddish cones of the female trees by insects. This is unique among conifers. Once pollinated, the females produce small winged seeds that are dispersed by the wind. These can lie dormant in the sand or in rocky crevices for many years before germinating.

This ancient welwitschia is estimated to be over 1,500 years old, yet stands just 1.5m (5ft) tall.

Ancient survivors of the Namib Desert

The welwitschias are true survivors. Not only do they thrive in the demanding environment of the Namib Desert, but research has also shown that they can also live for thousands of years. Tests carried out on welwitschias using carbon-14 dating techniques have established the age of some of the trees. Certain larger individuals, with trunks measuring over 1m (3¼ft) at the crown, were found to be more than 2,000 years old, while even those of modest size were over 700 years old.

The very great age that the welwitschia may reach, like many other ancient tree species, may be part of its long-term survival strategy. It may be that climatic cycles are in operation in western Africa that should be measured in hundreds (if not thousands) of years. Undoubtedly, in the past, parts of Africa enjoyed far more rain than they do today, so it may be the case that the welwitschia is adapted to a cycle of climatic variation that is on too grand a scale for us to perceive.

Since rain is absent in the desert for three out of every four years, the welwitschia has adapted to maximize and conserve the little water that is available. Early researchers noted the long tap root and believed that it penetrated deep into the ground to draw up underground water. However, research has revealed that while the tap root is important during the four-yearly rains, the plant has developed a more ingenious way of collecting water. The welwitschia grows in a part of the Namib Desert that is subject to dense sea fogs all year round, and it is the condensation of the fog and heavy dews that provide the tree with its water. Specially adapted pores on the leaves trap the precious moisture from the air, while the tangle of torn leaves enables the water to be channelled on to the sand so that it can be absorbed by the plant's roots.

BELOW
Welwitschia is unique amongst conifers in being pollinated by insects.

Another of the welwitschia's survival strategies is to make itself unpalatable to grazing animals. The leaves and bark contain bitter compounds that deter most predators, although the black rhino has been known to eat the welwitschia from time to time. The tree also exudes a colourless resin from its leaves and stem, which protects it against most insects and diseases. However, the dwarf tree's most prominent inhabitant is the yellow and black pyrrhocorid bug (*Probergrothius sexpunctatus*), which has found a way round the welwitschia's defences and lives by sucking its sap.

One curious aspect of the welwitschia's botany is the ability of several plants living close together to fuse into larger 'graft complexes'. The English botanist H. H. W. Pearson wrote in 1909:

'Of three such united groups, one consisted of a solid mass of five plants – one male and four female. One of the female plants, occupying a central position, appeared as if longitudinally split from the crown downwards by the ingrowth of another. A second clump contained two females at least: they were so intimately united that details of individuals could not be made out. In a third group, the largest of the three, the number of constituent plants was quite indeterminable.'

BAOBAB
The upside-down tree

BOTANICAL NAME
Adansonia digitata and
other species.

DISTRIBUTION
A. digitata: most of the African
continent and Madagascar.
Madagascar only: *A. grandidieri*,
A. madagascariensis, *A. perrieri*,
A. rubrostipa, *A. suarezensis*,
A. za. Northern Australia only:
A. gregorii.

**OLDEST KNOWN LIVING
SPECIMEN**
The baobab with the largest
diameter was the Glencoe Baobab
in South Africa until 2009, when it
measured 15.9m (52ft) in diameter
at breast height. It was estimated
to be at least 3,000 years old. The
largest living baobab in volume
today, and probably the oldest, is
at Sagole in northern South Africa,
and is 13.7m (45ft) in diameter
and 47m (154ft) in circumference.

RELIGIOUS SIGNIFICANCE
Considered holy in some places,
and also to be the home of
important spirits.

MYTHICAL ASSOCIATIONS
Numerous, relating to its origin
(how it came to be the upside-
down tree) and its powers.

CONSERVATION STATUS
Classified on the IUCN Red List of
Threatened Species as follows:
A. digitata: not classified;
A. grandidieri: endangered (2006);
A. madagascariensis: threatened
(2011); *A. perrieri*: threatened
(2011); *A. rubrostipa*: near
threatened (2011); *A. suarezensis*:
endangered (2011);
A. za: near threatened (2011).

Rising out of the savannah grasses with its broad, grotesque trunk and squat stature, Africa's most famous and distinctive tree – the baobab – is a magnificently arresting sight. Often wider than it is high, and with root-like branches that are devoid of leaves for large parts of the year, the 'upside-down tree', as it is sometimes affectionately known, seems an entirely appropriate name for this curiosity.

First described by a European in 1592, in Prospero Alpini's *De plantis Aegypti liber* (Natural History of Egypt), the most common species of baobab, *Adansonia digitata*, astonished viewers over 400 years ago. Growing over a large proportion of the African continent, this baobab – which is also known as Judas's bag and the monkey-bread tree – occurs as far north as Sudan and as far south as Northern Cape province in South Africa, and from the Cape Verde Islands in the west to

Ethiopia and Madagascar in the east. Altogether there are eight species of baobab: six of them occur only on the island of Madagascar, while one other species grows only in northern Australia.

A Caliban of a tree, a grizzled, distorted old goblin with the girth of a giant, the hide of a rhinoceros, twiggy fingers clutching at empty air.

HILARY BRADT, *GUIDE TO MADAGASCAR*

The largest authenticated baobab alive today in total volume stands at Sagole in the Northern Cape province and measures an astounding 13.7m (45ft) in diameter. However, the record for the largest diameter was held by the Glencoe Baobab, which had a vast trunk measuring 15.9m (52ft) until it split in 2009. The current record holder for diameter, according to the South African Dendrological Society, is the Sunland Baobab, located in Limpopo province, which has a diameter of 10.64m (35ft). At 22m (72ft) high, and with a circumference of some 47m (154ft), this baobab is slightly smaller, overall, than the Sagole tree. Radiocarbon dating has suggested that this giant may be up to 6,000 years old, and that there have been regular fires in its hollow trunk at least as far back as the year 1650. The enormous hollow inside the Sunland Baobab was turned into a pub and wine cellar in 1993 and has since become a popular tourist destination.

Some experts now believe that it is entirely possible that even larger trees existed in the past. An interesting feature of the baobab, which can make the precise recording of its dimensions more challenging, is that its trunk may fluctuate in size between seasons, as water is stored or used up.

The French botanist Michel Adanson (1727–1806) ascribed ages to some of the trees he had seen that were considered by many to be sacrilegious. His greatest estimate for an individual tree was 6,000 years. This implied that it must have begun life before the great flood of the Old Testament, then commonly believed to have taken place only 4,000 years before. Most scientists of the time disagreed with Adanson's calculations, but recent studies of tree rings and carbon-dated material taken from living trees have demonstrated that baobabs can indeed live to very great ages. A tree with a girth of just 4.5m (14¾ft), for example, has been shown to be over 1,000 years old. While the exact ages of most of the greatest baobabs of Africa have not been calculated, estimates based on the above information point to ages of more than 4,000 years for some. Research into the ages of the boab tree of Australia (*A. gregorii*) suggests that it too can reach ages in excess of 2,000 years. In the absence of scientific studies, the true ages of most of Madagascar's baobabs can only be guessed at. However, we know – from studies of the great ages reached by bristlecone pines and yew trees, for instance – that challenging growing conditions can produce trees of great age, if not great size, and thus some relatively small baobabs could still be immensely old.

The botany of Africa's most common baobab (*A. digitata*) is fascinating. It is not usually a tall tree, reaching only 14–23m (45–75ft) in height, but it is famous for its gigantic girth. The main trunk is generally cylindrical in shape and suddenly

A large double-trunked baobab standing in the savannah grasslands of Namibia.

tapers into a number of comparatively small, thin, spreading branches. Baobabs are deciduous trees and new foliage usually appears in late spring or early summer. The leaves of *A. digitata* take the form of five to seven leaflets, which look like fingers on a hand, giving rise to its botanical term 'digitata'. They produce large, sweet-scented white flowers, some 13–18cm (5–7in) wide, which are pollinated by a variety of nocturnal creatures, including bats and bushbabies. The egg-shaped fruits that form are covered with a green velvety skin, which makes them look rather like velvet purses dangling from the branches. The thick, woody shell of the fruit encases a pulpy white flesh in which a number of black seeds are set. This edible fruit is particularly relished by baboons, giving rise to one of the baobab's popular names: monkey-bread tree.

A tree of life

To many of the native peoples of Africa the baobab has not simply been a familiar feature of the savannah landscape but, literally, a 'tree of life'. Its special ability to store water during droughts has enabled many settled communities and nomadic peoples to survive, even though they may be far from any river system. Over thousands of years, the distribution of these strange trees has facilitated the expansion of great African nations such as the Bantu.

The baobab's enormous trunk acts as a water-storage organ: the largest baobabs can contain more than 136,000 litres (30,000 gallons) of water. Many

African peoples learnt long ago how to make use of this all-important feature.
The Kalahari bushmen, for example, have traditionally used the hollow stems of
grasses joined together, like straws, to reach the water inside the trunk, from where
it can be sucked out. In Sudan, however, some large baobab trunks are deliberately
hollowed out so that they will collect rainwater during the rainy season.

The baobab is remarkable not only for its water-storing properties: it also
provides a number of very useful products that have become central to the way
of life of numerous people. Once the bark has been cut away from the trunk, an
inner bast layer is revealed that yields a strong fibre used for making ropes, sacks
and nets, and which is even woven to make cloth. Other uses include the strings for
musical instruments and waterproof hats. Fortunately, baobabs have a remarkable
ability to regenerate and can survive the removal of large areas of bark.

The egg-shaped fruits of the baobab have been a traditional source of nutrition.
The woody shell encloses seeds set in a fleshy pulp, both of which can be eaten. The
pulp has a pleasant, tart flavour and, when dried, can be mixed with water to make

a refreshing drink. The fruit contains citric and tartaric acids, which are important to the diet of nomadic peoples. These acids have also been used by herding peoples in Africa to coagulate milk, and commercially to coagulate rubber.

The baobab's seeds – which are high in protein and oil – are generally either eaten on their own or mixed with millet to form a kind of gruel. They may also be pounded into a paste, like peanut butter, or traded for the extraction of their oil. Other parts of the tree that are edible include the young shoots put out by germinating seedlings, which are eaten like asparagus. Young leaves are also sometimes used in salads and provide important fodder for domesticated and wild animals alike. In Northern Cape province, in South Africa, caterpillars that live on the baobabs are also gathered as a food by the local people.

The trunk of the baobab tends to become hollow with old age, but in some areas people have assisted nature by hollowing out the trees themselves. Many ancient trees have considerable cavities of this kind inside them and, over the centuries, some extraordinary and ingenious uses have been made of this feature. The hollow inside the tree has proved to be an ideal place to store grain, water or even livestock, while people have even been known to set up home in larger baobabs. In Senegal, many hollows have been used as municipal buildings, sometimes with the badges of office carved into the outer trunk.

'We were lost in amazement, truly, at the stupendous grandeur of this mighty monarch of the forest … The dimensions of which we took with a measuring tape proved its circumference at its base to be twenty-nine yards. It had shed all its leaves (this was winter), but bore fruit from five to nine inches long, containing inside a brittle shell seeds and fibres like those of the tamarind, enclosed in a white acetic powder … which mixed with water makes a very pleasant drink.'

JAMES CHAPMAN, *TRAVELS IN THE INTERIOR OF SOUTH AFRICA* (1868)

OPPOSITE
The vast hollows that develop inside the trunks of many ancient baobab trees have been put to many uses including prisons, grain stores and even a bar.

BELOW
Large baobab trees near villages are considered important by local people, who often believe that they provide a meeting place for the ancestors and other spirits.

Baobabs have a long history of use, over thousands of years, for medicinal purposes. In some parts of Africa their bark is still used for the treatment of fevers and, for a time in Europe, it was used in place of cinchona bark (the source of quinine) in order to fight malaria. Because they are rich in vitamin C and calcium, the leaves and fruit also act in a preventative capacity against certain illnesses. Baobab pulp is burnt in some areas so that the smoke will fumigate the insects that live on domestic cattle.

Myths and legends

It is not surprising that a tree of such imposing stature as the baobab, and one that has become so important to so many different cultures, should have become the focus of numerous myths, legends and superstitions. A large number of beliefs about the baobab were collected by anthropologists and explorers at the beginning of the twentieth century. In both East and West Africa it was noted that mischievous spirits were believed to reside in the trees. In the Northern Cape province of South Africa, for example, it is still believed by some that spirits inhabit the large, white flowers and that anyone who plucks them will be eaten by a lion. In Senegal and Gambia, a tradition of placing the dead bodies of poets, musicians and 'buffoons' inside baobabs was also recorded. These people were believed to be possessed by demons and could therefore cause bad luck to befall crops or fisheries if they were buried in the ground or at sea. In Burkina Faso, the West African writer Seydou Dramé witnessed and wrote about the funeral of a baobab, noting that: 'Not all trees have a right to such treatment. The only ones are those that have played an important role in the life of the village, providing a resting place for local gods and a secret meeting place for the ancestors.'

The story of the upside-down tree

The following legend, of which there are numerous variations, comes from the slopes of Mount Kilimanjaro in Kenya. It explains how the baobab came to look as it does today.

A long, long time ago, a baobab stood beside a small pond and raised up its branches towards the sky. It looked at the other trees, whose crowns were covered in flowers, delicate bark and leaves. They shimmered with colour and the baobab saw all of this in the surface of the pond – like a mirror – and became angry. His own leaves were very small and his flowers scarcely visible. He was fat and his bark resembled the wrinkled skin of an old elephant. The tree called up to God and pleaded with him.

However, God had created the baobab and was satisfied with his work because this tree was unlike the other trees. He liked diversity. But he couldn't bear criticism. He asked the tree if it found the hippopotamus beautiful, and if it liked the cry of the hyena. Then God went back up into the sky to reflect in peace.

The baobab didn't stop looking at himself in the mirror, or complaining. So God came down again, seized the baobab, lifted him up and replanted him upside down in the earth. After this the baobab no longer looked at himself in the mirror, or complained again. Everything was restored to order.

Madagascan mystery

It is a curious fact that
only one baobab species,
A. digitata, is found across
the entire continent of
Africa, but that this species
and six others are found on
the island of Madagascar,
with a separate species
only in Australia. It has
been suggested that after
Madagascar separated
from mainland Africa 150
million years ago, either
unusual evolutionary
conditions gave rise to
the additional five species
or that all six species
were able to survive
because of the lack of
large herbivores. Another
theory is proposed by Dr
A. Baum, Professor of
Botany at the University
of Wisconsin, who studied
the chromosomes and the
structure of the flowers
of the different species.
The results suggested
that the genus *Adansonia*
evolved relatively recently
– between 7 and 17 million
years ago, long after the
continents had separated.
His theory is that the
large seeds, with their
waterproof shells, sailed
west to mainland Africa
and east to Australia on
ocean currents. However,
the seed pod of *A. gregorii*
(the Australian species)
is unique in not having a
waterproof shell. Baum
explains this as a recent
evolutionary change.

KAURI
Lord of the forest

BOTANICAL NAME
Agathis australis

DISTRIBUTION
Northern North Island,
New Zealand.

OLDEST KNOWN LIVING
SPECIMEN
Te Matua Ngahere in Waipoua
Forest: estimated over 2,000 years.

LARGEST SPECIMEN
Tane Mahuta: 45.2m (148ft 5in.);
diameter at breast height 4.91m
(16ft); total volume 516.7 cu. m
(18,250 cu. ft).

RELIGIOUS SIGNIFICANCE
Believed to possess its own spirit,
and revered by the Maori people.

MYTHICAL ASSOCIATIONS
Likened by the Maoris to the
whale, because of its huge size and
the smoothness of its bark.

CONSERVATION STATUS
Classified on the IUCN Red
List in 2000 as 'lower risk' and
'conservation-dependent'.

With their massive columnar trunks and elegant tracery of branches, the kauri trees of New Zealand give an unmistakable character to the North Island valleys and ridges they once dominated, and have inspired some who have observed them to liken them to Gothic cathedrals. Clearly distinct from the other trees that make up the subtropical rainforest around them, they rival the giant redwoods of California in size, and the largest individuals alive today are believed to be more than 2,000 years old.

These giants belong to an extremely ancient family of trees, the Araucariaceae, which were abundant before the coming of the dinosaurs and the break-up of the super-continent Gondwana. Although there are 13 other species and two subspecies of kauri, which grow in the tropical regions of Australia, Melanesia, New Guinea, the Philippines, the Celebes, Borneo, Sumatra and the Malay peninsula, the southern kauri (*Agathis australis*) is found only in New Zealand. More distant relatives of the kauri include the monkey puzzle and parana pine of South America and the Norfolk Island pine. In the far north of New Zealand's North Island are

swamplands where large kauri trees that were growing some 30–50,000 years ago have been discovered, preserved underwater.

Before the arrival of Europeans, kauri forest covered an estimated 1.6 million ha. (6177 sq. miles) of New Zealand's North Island. It was Captain Cook's excited reference to the forests he saw in 1769 that attracted the first European timber men. Cook (1728–79) noted: 'The banks of the river were completely clothed with the finest timber my eyes have ever seen.'

The arrival of the timber men, however, was to spell disaster both for the kauri trees and for the Maori people, who revered the trees. What followed was the wholesale destruction of the ancient and majestic kauri forests: in just 150 years they were to shrink to an area of barely 7,455 ha. (29 sq. miles). By the latter half of the twentieth century, however, people had come to appreciate the intrinsic value of the kauri forests once more. Today there are a number of refuges where the remaining giants are protected for posterity.

Kauri trees can grow to an immense size. Although the list of 'greatest' trees has changed as new discoveries and measurements have been made, today the tree estimated to have the broadest trunk and to be the oldest is in Waipoua Forest. It is known by its Maori name of Te Matua Ngahere, or Father of the Forest. Its trunk is 16.76m (55ft) in girth and it is free of branches for 10.2m (33ft) from the ground. The total height of the tree was nearly 37.4m (123ft) until it was severely damaged by strong storm winds in July 2007, which blew down the rata tree (*Metrosideros robusta*) that was growing within its crown as well as the top of the central trunk. Not far away, also in the Waipoua Forest, is Tane Mahuta or Lord

The smooth trunk regularly sheds flakes of bark, preventing the growth of epiphytes.

of the Forest, the largest standing kauri tree. Despite having a narrower trunk than Te Matua Ngahere – measuring 15.44m (50ft 8in) in girth – it is much taller at 45.2m (148ft 5in), and its massive trunk rises for nearly 18m (59ft) before the first branch appears. Its total volume is calculated to be an astonishing 516.7 cu. m (18,250 cu. ft).

Historical timber records suggest that there may have been a number of kauris that were even larger than the trees that survive today. An individual known as Kairaru stood on the slopes of Tutamoe, above Kaihu in Northland, which was estimated to have been about three times the size of Tane Mahuta before it was destroyed by forest fire in the 1880s. If this was true it would have been larger in volume than the greatest giant redwoods today. Te Matua Ngahere is reckoned (by counting the ring sequences from felled trees of equal girth) to be over 2,000 years old, but it is possible that Kairaru could have been more than 4,000 years old by the time it was destroyed.

The kauri forest

New Zealand's kauri forests developed only in the area of North Island, which has a warm, subtropical climate. Part of the rich and varied community of trees that flourished here, kauris did not cover large, continuous areas, but tended to form pockets or groves within the rainforests or coastal forests of the region. These forests held a number of other giant tree species, most notably Podocarpus species such as totara (*Podocarpus totara*), rimu (*Dacrydium cupressinum*) and kahikatea (*Dacrycarpus dacrydioides*).

The kauris also developed in association with a number of other tree species present today, and with vines and shrubs, which form a tangled understorey. Tall grasses, such as astelia and ghania sedge, grass trees, ferns and orchids are also typical. Young kauris sometimes compete with, and eventually overtake, copper-coloured celery pines at the edges of the forests. The shade cast by the giant kauris as they develop, and the nutrient-poor soils surrounding them, tend to prevent other large trees from becoming established nearby.

A curious feature of kauri trees, which are a kind of ancient conifer, is that as they develop they change shape as well as size. As a young 'ricker', in adolescence, the tall, thin-stemmed tree grows rapidly, assuming a narrow, conical shape. As it approaches maturity – at about **100–120** years old – it begins to develop a distinctive crown. Soon after the crown has begun to form, the lower limbs die back and fall off, leaving the smooth grey trunk that typifies an ancient kauri tree. The crown continues to fan out, eventually becoming an immense framework of branches. To support this top-heavy shape, deep tap roots extend for many metres

ABOVE
When the bark of a kauri tree is damaged it exudes a resinous gum that congeals in lumps as a defence against infection and wood-boring insects.

OPPOSITE
Kauri trees tend to live on nutrient-poor soils, in which small shrubs and hardy grasses form the understorey.

into the ground and develop knob-like structures at the tree's base to provide a lot of extra stability.

As the tree reaches a great age – many hundreds of years old – the trunk often becomes hollow, but new roots develop and form a direct link between the crown and the ground by passing down through the inside of the tree. In this way the kauris are able to flourish into old age.

Perhaps the most remarkable feature of the tree is its smooth, grey, branchless trunk – the sides being almost parallel until the branching crown is reached. The kauri has developed an ingenious way of remaining clear of parasitic plants, by simply shedding plates of its mottled bark whenever an unwanted guest tries to attach itself. Conversely, the tree's huge crown supports a number of epiphytic plants, including ferns and orchids, as well as other trees.

In order to reproduce, pollen from male catkins must come into contact with the female cones, which are green and about the size of a golf ball. In the autumn, the tiny winged seeds are ejected from the cones while they are still on the tree, but they can survive in this state for only a few days. A few seeds that fall onto suitable soils, in areas where there is sufficient light to enable them to germinate, will be successful. Some are carried by the wind to the edges of the grove, where favourable conditions are more likely to be found. However, the majority fall onto the thick leaf litter that carpets the forest floor beneath them, where they perish.

When he [a Maori] enters the forest he is among the offspring of Tane the Fertilizer, from whom he is also descended. He is among his own kindred, the descendants of the elder branch of his family, begotten by their common ancestor Tane, and under his protection. Thus when a man of the younger branch wishes to slay a member of the elder branch – that is to say, when he desires to fell a tree – it is necessary that he should avert ill consequences by a placation of Tane, the progenitor of trees and of man.

ELSDEN BEST, *THE MAORI CANOE*

Kauri timber and gum

Merchants of the British Navy and from Sydney began the trade in kauri timber some 200 years ago. The kauris that grew close to natural harbours were the first to be exploited and became highly sought after by traders, for use as masts and spars for sailing ships and later for house-building. The trees were so large that a single kauri could provide enough material for the construction of six houses. And honey-coloured kauri wood proved to be just as good for making furniture as it was for joinery. As the supply became exhausted, however, the search for timber moved inland. A timber industry quickly became established and it was the kauri that became the preferred building material in the countries bordering the Pacific. While kauri timber had formed a huge industry by the end of the nineteenth century, the resinous sap produced by the tree – known as kauri gum – was to become, in time, an even more valuable export. In Victorian times, some of the best-grade fossilized gum was used to make amber beads and jewellery; softer gum was suitable for carving into trinkets. In a living tree, kauri gum is exuded from natural wounds in the branches or bark, congealing in lumps to provide a defence against wood-boring insects and infections. The gum often accumulates in the crown of the tree and also in the roots. Once exposed to the air, or buried in the ground over long periods of time, the resin becomes very hard. The technique of bleeding gum from living trees was widely practised in the past. This caused considerable damage to the trees, however, often resulting in their death. Fossil kauri gum was produced by long-vanished trees – the result of being buried in the ground and hardening over thousands of years. Digging for fossil gum became a laborious occupation for large numbers of people, and in the 1890s some 20,000 individuals were involved. A major use for both gums was in the manufacture of high-grade varnish and, later, linoleum.

But the use of kauri gum pre-dates the arrival of European settlers by many centuries. The Maori had long been using *kapia*, as it was known. One of its uses was as a stain to colour *mokos*, or tattoos. Hardened gum was burnt and then ground to produce a fine, powdery soot, which was mixed with shark oil or animal fat to produce a blue-black or greenish pigment. Early tattoo techniques involved pricking the skin and rubbing in the coloured soot-and-oil mixture. When the wound had healed, a deep blue-green stain remained. In the early nineteenth century, a technique of actually carving the skin was developed, using tiny chisels that were dipped into the stain and then tapped directly on to the skin.

A Maori perspective

The Maori believe that they live in a world in which nothing is inanimate. All natural objects possess a spirit and share a common ancestry with them. All are considered to be descended from the Sky Father and the Earth Mother. When a tree was to be felled – the trees were used chiefly for canoes, meeting houses and shrines – the Maori observed solemn ceremonies and offered up incantations, because the giant kauris were considered to be their elders who, like themselves, were under the protection of Tane Mahuta, the supreme being.

The felling of a tree was not undertaken lightly. Once the kauri had been selected and the work party prepared, other vitally important decisions had to be made: the tohunga (wise men or priests) were consulted about the best day to start, and the state of the moon was considered too; choosing the wrong day to begin might cause the canoe to capsize, the war party using it to be defeated, or no fish to be caught.

For many Maori people today, protecting the forests also means protecting the home of their ancestors and retaining a vital part of their cultural heritage for the generations to come – the descendants of Tane Mahuta, the Lord of the Forest. Now protected in a number of forest reserves, the kauri is being assisted to regenerate in various ways. The long-term aim is to re-create more magnificent kauri groves, set in a mosaic of forest habitats that are typical of New Zealand's North Island.

> *We travelled through a wood so thick that the light of heaven could not penetrate the trees that composed it. Not a gleam of sky was to be seen. All was a mass of gigantic trees, straight and lofty, their wide-spreading branches meeting overhead and producing an endless darkness.*
>
> AUGUSTUS EARLE, *A NARRATIVE OF A NINE MONTHS' RESIDENCE IN NEW ZEALAND IN 1827*

BELOW
The Maori believe that all natural objects possess a spirit and that protecting the kauri forest today protects the home of their ancestors.

TOTARA
Sacred tree of the Maoris

BOTANICAL NAME
Podocarpus totara

DISTRIBUTION
North Island and South Island,
New Zealand.

OLDEST KNOWN LIVING
SPECIMEN
The Pouakani tree, on North
Island, is believed to be 1,800
years old, and is 3.8m (12.7ft) in
diameter at breast height, 42.7m
(140ft) tall.

RELIGIOUS SIGNIFICANCE
Believed to have a spirit, and a
common ancestry with the Maori
people, and therefore to be an
elder of living Maoris.

CONSERVATION STATUS
Classified on the IUCN Red List
of Threatened Species in 1998
as of 'lower risk/least concern'.
Many of the largest trees are now
in protected areas. Trees occur
widely across both North and
South Islands.

PREVIOUS PAGE
A large totara growing in the
Pureora Forest on North
Island, New Zealand.

OPPOSITE
A detail of the intricate totara carving
that adorns the Waitangi Meeting
House near Paihia.

BELOW
The Pouakani tree near the Pureora
Forest reserve is 42.7m (140ft)
tall and estimated to be
around 1,800 years old.

The totara (*Podocarpus totara*) is one of New Zealand's most magnificent and culturally important trees, and once formed part of the huge forests that clothed both North and South Islands before the arrival of the first Europeans. Today it is still widely distributed across both islands, but in very much reduced numbers. One of the finest remnants of native forest on North Island is to be found in the Pureora Forest Reserve, which straddles the Hauhungaroa Range, west of Lake Taupo and east of Te Kuiti. Towering above the verdant tangle of mosses, ferns, small shrubs and epiphytic growth that form the understorey are some true forest giants, which include totara trees.

The totara belongs to an extremely ancient tree family, the Podocarpaceae, which was thriving long before the islands that comprise New Zealand had separated from the continents of South America, Australasia, Africa and Asia around 150 million years ago. Fossil records show that in New Zealand, members of this family have remained virtually unchanged botanically over the past 70 million years.

The totara can attain a great age. One of the largest and oldest examples is the tree known as Pouakani, located on the western side of Pureora mountain. It has a diameter at breast height of 3.8m (12.7ft) and rises to a height of some 42.7m (140ft). By studying felled trees of a similar size whose growth rings have been counted, experts believe the tree to be around 1,800 years old. Investigation of ancient tree stumps has suggested that totaras are able to live to beyond 2,000 years old.

The tree and its forest

The totara is a tall, elegant tree with a straight, branch-free trunk for much of its height. It has a grey or reddish bark, which appears thick, stringy and furrowed. A conifer, the totara's leaves and fruit resemble those of yew trees (*Taxus* species) since they have narrow, needle-like leaves accompanied by bright red fleshy fruits. There are separate male and female trees and, as they age, the foliage becomes increasingly sparse.

Today, the totara is regularly found growing in association with native rimu (*Dacrydium cupressinum*), matai (*Prumnopitys taxifolia*) and miro (*Prumnopitys ferruginea*) trees, especially on soils that are high in volcanic ash and

Uses of the totara

Totara trees were the species most commonly used for timber by the Maori. The most important uses of the wood were for carvings and for making and decorating war and fishing canoes, and for the construction of domestic houses and *marae*, or ceremonial meeting houses. Strips of bark were also used to attach thatching to house frames. Totara is still used for Maori ceremonial objects and for making bowls and other items. The wood is relatively easy to work, but only small amounts of carving can be undertaken at any one time due to its tendency to split.

172

therefore well drained. The remnants of
the great podocarp forests support
abundant bird life such as the kereru,
tui, fantail, wax-eye and kaka. There are
also populations of the rare New Zealand
falcon, blue duck and North Island
robin, and one of the largest remaining
populations of the kokako.

In some cases a man might repeat a charm over such a reserved tree in order
to preserve it from the elements … lest it be destroyed by Tawhiri-matea
[the Maori god of weather].

ELSDEN BEST, *THE MAORI CANOE*

Over the last 200 years, the
native forests have largely been destroyed in North Island, first for timber for
construction and shipbuilding and more recently to make way for commercial
plantations. This practice continued until the 1970s, and had it not been for a
series of tree-top protests in 1978, many of the most ancient totara trees and even
more native podocarp forest would have been destroyed. One of the results of the
protests and campaigning was the setting up of the Pureora Forest Reserve and the
saving of the magnificent Pouakani tree.

The Maoris and the totara

Totara timber was greatly favoured by the Maori and used for a variety of
purposes, from everyday house-building to ceremonial carvings. The Maori were
extremely skilful when working with wood: an experienced carver or boat-builder
could tell, simply by looking at a totara tree standing in the forest, whether it
would be suitable for the purpose he had in mind. The totara was so highly prized
that, when a good tree was located, the underbrush would be cleared in advance
of its use, as a sign that it was already reserved. The tree might then be left to
continue growing for many years before it was finally used.

Sometimes, when a suitable tree for canoe-building was found, a strip of bark
was peeled off the trunk to induce the tree to rot, making the hollowing-out process
much easier when the totara was eventually felled. Well-known individuals or
groups of totaras were often given names. For example, the tree from which the
famous 'Takitimu' canoe was carved was known as Te Puwenua.

Maori canoes were vitally important both for warfare and as a means of
procuring food. The tree that was to become the *hiwi*, or hull, was selected from
an area that was considered to have good omens. Special chants were used by the
tohunga, or priest, to improve the good fortune of the finished boat. Specific trees
were sometimes even the cause of warfare between two tribes. A special tree might
also be left as an heirloom for a son or grandson.

OPPOSITE
Totara forest at Arthur's Pass, South
Island. Totara trees occur on both
North Island and South Island.

Rata's waka

This is the Maori story of what happened to Rata, who wanted to cut down a totara tree but had not asked permission from Tane Mahuta, Lord of the Forest.

Long ago, Rata was wandering sadly along the bank of a stream, thinking about his father, who had just died. 'I must bring him home,' thought Rata, 'but how am I going to do that?'

He stared at the trees in the forest and said to himself, 'I need a waka, a canoe big enough to hold many warriors.'

He walked through the forest looking for a suitable tree. 'Miro … rimu … kahikatea … tanekaha … totara. Yes, totara it shall be.'

Early the next morning, Rata returned to the forest and chopped down the totara tree. The next day, when he returned, the tree trunk was no longer lying on the ground. Rata stared at the trees around him and, with a start, recognized the totara that he had felled: it was growing tall and proud again, as though it had never been touched. Rata was puzzled and a little fearful. He took up his axe and began to chop down the totara tree again. The following morning he found it again standing tall and silent. For a third time Rata chopped it down. He shaped it and began to scoop out the inside. When night fell, he left the half-formed canoe and went home.

Later that night, he took down his fighting spear and quietly stole back to the forest. As he approached, he could hear strange singing and see light shining through the trees. He held his breath and crept closer. Then he stared in amazement. Birds were scurrying backwards and forwards, carrying leaves and twigs in their beaks. Thousands of insects were swarming all over the log, replacing chips and filling up the hollow. As he watched, the half-formed canoe disappeared and was replaced by a smooth trunk that glowed red in the light.

Rata could not bear to be hidden any longer. He stood up and stepped into the light. At once the singing stopped and the light went out. Rata was alone. 'Come back', he whispered. 'I am sorry I cut down the totara tree. Please forgive me. I did not mean to harm it. I just wanted to build a canoe in order to fetch my father.'

He began to lift the heavy trunk. Then all at once he felt it move, turn slowly, lift off the ground and settle on the stump from which he had cut it. Rata put his arms around the tree. As he held on to it, he felt thousands of little legs running over his body and on to the tree trunk. But when the dawn came, Rata was alone. The totara was whole once more. 'I shall never cut down another tree again', vowed Rata.

'You may,' said a voice close to him, 'but you must ask Tane Mahuta, god of the forest and birds, for permission. He created all these trees and birds for Papatuanuku, the Earth Mother. Ask him when you want to use any of it.'

Rata turned to see who was speaking. There was no one beside him. As he prepared to leave, his heart leapt as he saw a war canoe. 'Mine?' he whispered.

'Yes,' replied the voice, 'Rata's waka.'

ANTARCTIC BEECH
Survivor from Gondwana

BOTANICAL NAME
Nothofagus moorei

DISTRIBUTION
South-eastern Queensland and
north-eastern New South Wales,
Australia, from the headwaters of
the Manning River north to the
McPherson Range.

**OLDEST KNOWN LIVING
SPECIMEN**
Estimated at between 1,000–
3,000 years old.

CONSERVATION STATUS
Not yet classified on the IUCN
Red List of Threatened Species.

Looming through the cool mists that shroud remote, rainforest-covered mountain tops and ridges in eastern Australia, the majestic Antarctic beech (*Nothofagus moorei*), with its moss-covered trunks and branches, is one of Australia's most venerable trees. With crooked, shaggy limbs that reach out like arms and fingers, a grove of ancient Antarctic beeches is an arresting sight, conjuring up the image of a secret world, a mythical landscape, lost in time. These beautiful trees, now rare outside the national parks in which they are protected, are found only in the south-eastern corner of Queensland, extending to the nearby North Coast and Northern Tablelands of north-eastern New South Wales.

Maturing very slowly, the Antarctic beech gives the impression of being not one but several trees. Various trunks of different sizes are often joined together at their bases, in coppice formation, having grown up in a ring around what was once the parent trunk. Generally found leaning, and often gnarled with large burrs, they have a sculptural quality that implies great age.

Antarctic beeches do not appear to reach an enormous girth – about 3m (10ft) seems to be the maximum size for an individual trunk – but they may reach over 50m (164ft) in height, and are believed to be able to live for at least 3,000 years. Needing cool temperatures and constant moisture to thrive, the Antarctic beech grows naturally only above 600m (1,970ft), and up to 1,550m (5,080ft) above sea level. Here, in the cool temperate rainforest, where rainfall is high and mists are common, it has evolved as a dominant species among the other rainforest trees, preferring the banks of streams and deep gullies, as well as mountain ridges, as its habitat. Not surprisingly, a former common name for this impressive tree was 'mountain beech'. The areas in which the Antarctic beech is found are characterized by a very low density of other tree species: sometimes only three may be present, but often only one.

Rising up from a forest floor that is largely carpeted with ferns of different kinds, the trunk and branches of the Antarctic beech are mostly concealed by the plethora of other plants that depend on them. Wiry vines, small ferns, mosses, lichens and orchids festoon their crooked trunks and branches. Referring to the

Antarctic beeches he had seen growing in the region of the Dorrigo Mountain in New South Wales, the British-born Australian botanist J. H. Maiden (1859–1925) wrote in 1894, 'No tree in the brush surpasses it in the quantity of epiphytal vegetation it supports.'

Beneath its mantle of mosses and other vegetation, the trunk of the Antarctic beech has a scaly, porous, dark red bark, though it turns dark brown when dead and is shed in large, irregular patches. Its twigs and small branches are covered with a brownish down. An evergreen, the tree has glossy, dark green leaves that are lance-shaped and finely toothed towards their tips. They feel rigid and leathery to the touch and are brittle in texture. The tree has a compact crown and is seldom without some red or orange-coloured dying leaves. New spring growth, however, is a deep red.

It was this dramatic coloration that gave rise to an earlier name for the tree – red beech – and the name by which its timber has been traded, the Negrohead beech.

Nothofagus moorei is one of a number of related (*Nothofagus*) tree species, commonly referred to as southern beech, that are native to parts of the southern hemisphere. Here they have become important timber trees – in this respect being second only to the eucalyptus. Because of their similarity to the beeches of the northern hemisphere, botanists have traditionally described them as part of the tree family to which true beeches (the Fagaceae) belong. Recent research, however, has supported the view that they are in fact much more closely related to the birch family (the Betulaceae) and botanists now place them in a family of their own: the Nothofagaceae.

Discovery of the Antarctic beech

The Antarctic beech is a survivor from the remote past. Over 200 million years ago, the Antarctic continent was covered in luxuriant vegetation and formed part of the super-continent Gondwana. Fossil evidence from core samples taken from the ice below Antarctica shows that this vegetation included relatives of the *Nothofagus* species that survive in the southern hemisphere today.

Undoubtedly known to, and held in deep respect by, the Aborigine groups who once made use of the Australian forests in which these trees live, the Antarctic beech has taken its formal botanical name from the British botanist Charles Moore (1820–1905), who was appointed government botanist and director of the Botanic Gardens in Sydney by the Colonial Office in London in 1848.

He set about restoring the scientific character of the botanic gardens, which had become neglected, and, as an avid collector, travelled widely. Moore had a particular interest in the timber trees of Queensland and New South Wales, including the Antarctic beech. This tree had first been 'discovered' by a Mr Carron and a Mr W. A. B. Greaves, on the Upper Clarence River in New South Wales, in

An ancient partnership
Over thousands of years
the rainforest has come
to present a complex,
delicate interaction
between a vast array of
living organisms. The
majestic Antarctic beech
has become the host
for a variety of mosses,
ferns and other epiphytic
plants, but for one plant
it has become almost
its only home. This is
the beautiful epiphytic
orchid *Dendrobium
falcorostrum*, one of
the largest orchids to
be found in the cool
temperate rainforests
of New South Wales. It
was once so common on
Antarctic beeches that
it was called the beech
orchid, but now it is, like
its host, rare in the wild.

1865. Moore named the Antarctic beech after Mr Carron, but it subsequently became one of the 19 species that were named after Moore himself (*Fagus carronii* C. Moore).

At the time that the Antarctic beech was first described (the end of the nineteenth century), the trees were much more numerous than they are today, forming dense forests on some of the high mountain slopes in New South Wales. Since it was a particularly slow-growing tree, however, the very hard timber that the Antarctic beech produced became highly sought after. In 1894, J. H. Maiden described the wood as follows:

'It is the hardest timber of the brush, and it is also very heavy … There is no doubt that it is a most durable timber … I would look upon it as a valuable timber for culverts and such situations, where it is liable to wet, and I trust that the authorities will give it a fair trial … Large trees throw out burrs, from which depend aerial roots. The timbers of these burrs often yield a beautiful figure.'

The fine and even-textured timber – red when freshly cut, but drying to a pinkish colour – was thereafter extensively used for a number of purposes, including piano construction, cabinet work and soft turnery.

Because of past felling activity and because regeneration of the young seedlings is so slow, the magnificent Antarctic beech is now rare in the wild. The timber is still traded, however, and has a high commercial value. Fortunately, a number of magnificent examples of this ancient tree are now protected in a number of national parks and forest reserves across its natural range.

Many of the trees are bent and gnarled. The very dark green foliage is striking, and the shape and habit of the leaves is handsome. Altogether, it is one of the most interesting of our forest trees.

J. H. MAIDEN, *AGRICULTURAL GAZETTE*, NEW SOUTH WALES, 1894

OPPOSITE
Antarctic beech trees grow in association with many types of epiphytes such as ferns, mosses and fungi.

FIG
Sacred tree of the Old World

BOTANICAL NAME
Ficus benghalensis (banyan tree)
Ficus carica (common fig)
Ficus religiosa (bo or bodhi tree)
Ficus sycomorus (sycamore fig)

DISTRIBUTION
Ficus species are found in all tropical and some temperate regions.

OLDEST KNOWN LIVING SPECIMEN
The bodhi tree at Anuradhapura, Sri Lanka is 2,300 years old.

RELIGIOUS SIGNIFICANCE
Banyan is sacred to many peoples in India, China and South East Asia; sycamore fig was sacred to the Ancient Egyptians; the bodhi tree is revered by Buddhists and Hindus.

MYTHICAL ASSOCIATIONS
Common fig venerated by the Romans for its associations with Romulus and Remus; banyan believed in both China and India to be the home of demons and tree spirits.

CONSERVATION STATUS
Not classified on the IUCN Red List of Threatened Species.

Few groups of trees have the religious significance of figs, and few have played such an important part in human history. Truly remarkable fig trees occur, mostly in tropical regions, all around the world: some are vast, with canopies measured in hectares; some are tropical rainforest giants that strangle their hosts; others are sacred to millions of people; and one individual said to have been planted in 288 BC is still thriving today.

There are some 750 species of fig in the world belonging to the Moraceae family. They are found in all tropical and some temperate regions, in countries as diverse as Mexico, China, New Zealand and Namibia. Fig trees vary enormously in size: while some are only a few metres tall when mature, others can reach heights of more than 45m (147ft) in tropical rainforests. They tend to be evergreen in tropical regions and deciduous in more temperate climates. One of the most famous kinds of fig is the strangler fig. It starts life as a tiny seedling in the crook of a branch high in the forest canopy, from where it extends roots downwards to reach nutrients in the soil of the forest floor. Gradually the roots wrap and widen around the trunk, until the host is eventually killed.

The fig tree features strongly in religious history and mythology in various parts of the world. The Romans venerated fig trees because, in the story of Romulus and Remus, their cradle became caught on the branches of a fig in a place that was to become Rome. In China, spirits were believed to live in large fig trees,

Pollination

Recent research into fig fossils by Dr Steve Compton of the University of Leeds in the UK has shown that the way in which wasps pollinate fig flowers has remained unchanged for at least 34 million years. Fossils found on the Isle of Wight in the UK show that prehistoric fig wasps used exactly the same parts of their bodies to carry pollen and to get inside figs as those living today. There are about 750 species of fig tree and each needs a specific miniature wasp (just 1.5mm long) to pollinate it.

while on the Indian subcontinent sizeable trees were thought to house demons. The sycamore fig (*Ficus sycomorus*) was, in the Bible lands, 'intimately connected with the rites and mysteries of ancient Nature-worship', as *Plants of the Bible* (Harold N. and Alma L. Moldenke, 1952) states. The common fig (*Ficus carica*) was the first plant to be mentioned by name in the Bible, as the source of the 'aprons' of leaves made by Adam and Eve to cover their nakedness. The common fig is referred to no fewer than 57 times in the Bible and is generally synonymous with self-sufficiency.

The banyan – crown of thorns

The banyan tree (*Ficus benghalensis*) is sacred to many peoples across the Indian subcontinent, the Himalayas, China and many parts of South East Asia. Individuals can grow to an extraordinary size, producing some of the world's most spectacular trees. The spreading canopy of the banyan can become so huge, that according to legend, Alexander the Great (356–323 BC) and his entire army were able to shelter under a single tree.

The most famous banyan in terms of size, known as the Great Banyan, is located in the Chandra Bose Botanic Garden near Kolkata, India. It started life in the canopy of a date palm growing in the botanic garden only some 200 years ago. From these humble beginnings, it has grown into what is generally regarded as the widest tree in the world. After a lightning strike in 1925, the middle of the tree was removed and, now looking more like a forest than a single tree, it has since formed a colony – composed of over 3,000 aerial roots. Occupying an enormous area of some 14,500 sq. m (156,077 sq. ft), the present crown has a circumference of about 1km (⅝ mile).

There are a number of banyan trees that are considerably older, and other examples of greater size. Perhaps the most remarkable of these is the one growing on the banks of the River Nebudda, east of Bombay. This tree has a truly colossal canopy, measuring an astounding 194m (637ft) in diameter, which is supported by 320 main stems and more than 3,000 smaller ones. It is virtually a one-tree forest.

There is a long history of belief in Asia that demons and spirits inhabit large trees, and banyan trees feature in many traditional stories. One Indian legend refers to a large banyan tree that was the home of a number of tree spirits, who were said to wring the neck of anyone who approached at night. In China, tree spirits were believed to manifest themselves as bulls, serpents and a number of other creatures. One of the most revered trees in China is the great Green Banyan of Ching.

Banyan figs – as well as the sycamore and common fig – were also known to Middle Eastern peoples in biblical times. Some scholars have proposed that the Tree of Life growing in the centre of the Garden of Eden was in fact a banyan.

Tree of knowledge

Ficus religiosa is known by a variety of names, most commonly 'bo' or 'bodhi'. It is a large, fast-growing deciduous tree, with a fluted trunk covered in a smooth grey bark. Unlike many other fig species, it does not have aerial roots and is not a strangler, but splits its host tree as it grows. It has large, heart-shaped leaves that taper to a point and these are set on long, slender stalks, causing the foliage to move in the lightest of breezes.

The bo is one of the most sacred trees in India, Sri Lanka and Nepal, where it is venerated by both Hindus and Buddhists. The individual known as 'the Bodhi Tree', which now grows at the Mahabodhi temple in Bodh Gaya in north-east India, is said to be a direct descendant of the tree under which Siddhartha Gautama, the founder of Buddhism, found enlightenment over 2,600 years ago. Images often depict this event, showing Buddha under a large, spreading bo tree, with demons attacking him on one side and vanquished demons escaping on the other. According to ancient tradition, the original bodhi tree at Bodh Gaya was nurtured by the earth goddess and, at the very moment of Buddha's enlightenment, all the flowering trees in the world burst into flower and became heavy with fruit. Buddhists regard the bodhi as the personification of Buddha.

The bo tree is also revered by Hindus, who have a strong religious objection to cutting it down. In the Hindu religion, Vishnu (the second member of the Hindu trinity) is said to have been born under a bo tree and is often depicted sitting on its heart-shaped leaves. The bo tree is often planted in the grounds of temples and, of all the sacred trees of India, it is the most widely worshipped.

The most famous sacred bo tree in Sri Lanka is located in Anuradhapura and is said to be the oldest tree in the world with a known planting date. This fig is said to have grown from a branch taken from the original bodhi tree in India under which Buddha received enlightenment; the branch was sent to King Devanampiyatissa by

The fig tree, not that for fruit renowned,
But such as at this day to Indians known
In Malabar or Deccan spreads her arms,
Branching so broad and long, that in the ground
The bended twigs take root, and daughters grow
About the mother tree …

JOHN MILTON, *PARADISE LOST*, IX, 1101–1106 (1667)

ABOVE
Sycamore figs were believed by
the Ancient Egyptians to line
the route to the afterlife.

OPPOSITE
Domesticated edible figs, such as
this one near Rimini, Italy, will not
produce fruit without the aid of
minute flightless wasps.

India's King Asoka in 288 BC. The king planted it and prophesied that it would thrive forever. Other bo trees found in temple gardens across Sri Lanka are all thought to be cuttings from the famous tree at Anuradhapura.

Tree of life and afterlife

The sycamore fig (*Ficus sycomorus*) is a robust, wide-spreading, semi-evergreen tree found in an area stretching from the Middle East, North and central Africa as far south as KwaZulu-Natal in southern Africa. Unlike the banyan, the sycamore fig does not spread out laterally with the aid of aerial roots. Instead, its main trunk, clad in pale brown papery bark, divides into numerous spreading branches close to the ground. It is not a tall tree, however, typically growing to just 9–12m (30–40ft), and large specimens have a spreading canopy of only about 36m (120ft) in diameter. The largest sycamore fig (and probably the oldest) stands in the Kruger National Park in South Africa. In comparison with other trees of known age, this fig must be well over 1,000 years old.

The sycamore fig was particularly important to the Ancient Egyptians, who revered impressive trees. It grew abundantly and was considered to be one of the two most sacred trees of Ancient Egypt. As such, it often featured in Egyptian sculptures and was occasionally represented as the 'tree of life'. A mythical sycamore fig even stood on the path to the afterlife, supplying food and drink to the souls of the dead on their journey to the Otherworld.

CEDAR
Tree of the gods

BOTANICAL NAME
Cedrus libani (cedar of Lebanon);
Cedrus brevifolia (sometimes
known as cedar of Cyprus);
Cedrus atlantica (Atlas or Algerian
cedar); *Cedrus deodara* (deodar)

DISTRIBUTION
Cedar of Lebanon: Lebanon, Syria
and Turkey. *Cedrus brevifolia*:
western Troodos Mountains,
Cyprus. Atlas or Algerian cedar:
Algeria and Morocco. Deodar:
western Himalayas, from northern
Pakistan and Afghanistan through
Kashmir to western Nepal.

**OLDEST KNOWN LIVING
SPECIMEN**
Cedar of Lebanon: ancient grove
on slopes of Mount Lebanon,
possibly 3,000 years. Deodar:
oldest verifiable tree around
1,500 years old.

RELIGIOUS SIGNIFICANCE
Cedar of Lebanon: revered by
ancient peoples of the Holy Land;
deodar: regarded as 'tree of the
gods' by Hindus in India.

CONSERVATION STATUS
Classified on the IUCN Red List
of Threatened Species in 1998:
C. libani and *C. atlantica*: 'lower
risk/least concern'; *C. brevifolia*
'vulnerable' (2011).

To many people, the cedars reign supreme among the conifers, unequalled for their majestic form and their aura of great antiquity. Whether at home in their native lands, or gracing the lawns of distinguished country houses, cedars stand out, seemingly timeless and immortal.

Many different conifers with dark, scented wood have been called 'cedars' in an attempt to classify them. In North America we find, among others, the western and eastern red cedars, and the incense and Alaskan cedars. In the Far East, the Chinese cedar and Japanese red cedar are two more species with misleading common names. There are, in fact, only four true cedars. Three of these are native to the Mediterranean region, while the fourth comes from the western Himalayas.

As its name suggests, the cedar of Lebanon (*Cedrus libani*) is indigenous to Lebanon, but also to Syria and the Taurus Mountains of Turkey. *Cedrus brevifolia* is found only on the island of Cyprus, where it has a very restricted habitat – a few valleys on the western side of the Troodos Mountains. The Atlas cedar (*Cedrus atlantica*) is a native tree of the Atlas Mountains in Algeria and Morocco, while the deodar (*Cedrus deodara*) grows naturally in the Himalayan region stretching from Pakistan and Afghanistan across northern India to western Nepal.

All these cedars are closely related, so much so that the botanist and explorer Sir Joseph Hooker (1817–1911), who was director of the Royal Botanic Gardens at Kew from 1865–85, thought that they should all be classified together as one species. Still, today, some botanists believe that the cedar found in Cyprus is only a geographical variation of the cedar of Lebanon. The main difference between the two species is the size of the needles: those of *Cedrus brevifolia*, as its name suggests, being slightly smaller than those of its neighbour on the mainland. In other respects, the trees are very similar.

Trees of the Lord

Cedars are the trees that are most often mentioned in the Bible, and most of these references are to the famous and much celebrated cedars of Lebanon, known in that country simply as *al Arz* (the cedars), or *al Arz ar Rab* (the cedars of the Lord). It is not difficult to see why the peoples of the Bible lands, including the

Israelites, should have held them in such high esteem and regarded them with reverence: cedars would certainly have been the most massive and noble trees with which they were acquainted and amongst the longest-lived. In the Bible, cedars are frequently used as symbols of might, power and dignity; of grandeur, prowess and glory; and of beauty and fruitfulness. In the Song of Songs, cedars are used to help evoke a fitting image of Christ himself: 'His countenance is as Lebanon, excellent as the cedars' (Song of Solomon 5:15).

An ancient biblical myth tells of an angel who took refuge beneath a massive cedar tree during a terrible storm. After the storm had abated, the angel prayed to God that this tree, whose wood was so fragrant and whose shade was so refreshing, would also in the future bear some fruit that would be useful to the human race. This fruit, according to the myth, was the sacred body of Jesus Christ. Another biblical story tells of Seth, the son of Adam, planting a cutting from the Tree of Life on Adam's grave. The cutting eventually grew into a tree with three branches: one of cypress wood, one of cedar and one of olive. The story relates that it was from this tree that the cross upon which Jesus was crucified was made.

Some 4,000km (2,500 miles) away to the east, the equally majestic deodar engendered similar feelings among the Hindu peoples of north-west India's Himalayan region. The name 'deodar' is derived from the Sanskrit *devadaru* or *deodaru*, and means literally 'tree of the gods'. The Himalayas, whose glaciers are the source of the sacred River Ganges, are said to be the home of the Hindu gods

Behold, the Assyrian was a cedar in Lebanon with fair branches, and with a shadowing shroud, and of a high stature; … the fir trees were not like his boughs, and the chestnut trees were not like his branches; nor any tree in the garden of God was like unto him in his beauty. I have made him fair by the multitude of his branches: so that all the trees of Eden, that were in the garden of God, envied him.

EZEKIEL (31:3, 8–9)

and some of their most sacred shrines are found here. The Indian god Shiva, his wife Parva and Vishnu the Preserver are all believed to live in this breathtakingly beautiful region.

The Indian state of Uttar Pradesh, in which extensive deodar forests are still to be found, contains India's highest mountain peaks. Forming what are often regarded as some of the most majestic of the world's forests, the deodar extends from parts of northern Pakistan and Afghanistan in the west through Kashmir in India to western Nepal. It grows in areas of the outer Himalayas where the full strength of the monsoon is felt, in the intermediate ranges and valleys, and also in arid zones deep within the Himalayas. The hardy deodar has colonized the middle slopes of some of the highest mountain ranges in the world. Throughout this region

this stately tree has long been esteemed (like its cousins in Lebanon and Turkey, and in North Africa) for its vigour and beauty and for the great size and age it can reach. To Hindus, the deodar is considered divine.

The Hebrew words for cedar, *erez* or *ahrahzim*, used in the Bible, are derived from an old Arabic term meaning 'firmly rooted and strong tree', and this expression could well be used to describe all the cedar species, especially when they reach maturity. While still young, cedars are roughly pyramidal in shape, but as they mature – after about 100 years – and if given the space, their tops flatten out and the branches take on a characteristic horizontal form, becoming large and wide-spreading. The results are impressive and beautiful, as they 'strike their splendid attitudes, forming black plateaux ... spreading a black table against the sky', as Hugh Johnson noted in his *Encylopedia of Trees*.

Few conifers are as graceful or elegant as the deodar, with its pendulous outer shoots, especially when it is young. Although it may develop the flat, spreading top of the Lebanon and Atlas cedars, it generally grows with a straight trunk, in the form of a slender spire. In the wild, its arched leading shoots assist the deodar in growing up through overhead branches of the forest understorey to become a dominant tree. The graceful pyramidal shape that the tree can maintain into maturity, and its weeping-tipped branches, make it easier to distinguish from other cedars. It also differs from the Lebanon and Atlas cedars by having longer needles, and young twigs that are distinctly more downy. The deodar is often, too, a taller tree than the other cedars, reaching some 76m (250ft) in the wild and with a girth of some 13.7m (45ft). Tree-ring analysis of a deodar in Lahaul, Himachal Pradesh, India, suggests that it is over 1,500 years old.

The majestic cedar of Lebanon tends to grow in coppice formation, sending up several gigantic trunks from the base at ground level, with enormous branches attached. It may reach some 39.6m (130ft) in height and achieve a diameter of around 4m (13ft). According to dendrologist Alan Mitchell (1922–95), the volume of timber contained in an ancient, large-branched, multi-stemmed specimen is comparable to that of 'the best coast redwoods and perhaps the giant sequoia'.

Growing in the wild in the country from which they have taken their popular name, the oldest cedars of Lebanon may be 3,000 years old, although cedar expert Dr Sawsan Khuri believes them to be around 1,000 years old. According to tree enthusiast Thomas Pakenham, the 'gnarled and tormented trees' he encountered in Turkey in 1993, which were reported to be older than those in Lebanon, were up to 1,000 years old. Since the largest trees (in the Lebanon) are hollow, exact calculations of their age are difficult to make. The largest deodars and Atlas cedars may also be around 1,000 years old.

Fragrant oils
The cedars are well known for the fragrant oils contained within their wood, which have been put to many different uses. With its warm, spicy fragrance, the oil that is extracted from the deodar is very popular in India and is used in traditional Ayurvedic medicine to treat fevers and pulmonary and urinary disorders, among other maladies. In modern aromatherapy it is used for dermatitis, hair loss and nervous tension, and it is said to enhance meditative relaxation and relieve stress.

Trees of beauty, trees of utility

It is not just the beauty and longevity of the cedars that singled them out for special attention in antiquity. Their fragrant wood was greatly prized for its remarkable durability, the ease with which it could be worked, and the enormous size of the timbers that could be cut from it.

The deodar's timber is the strongest of those produced by the conifers native to India, and one of the country's most important timber trees. The fragrant oil present in its wood (which turns yellowish-brown after cutting) has given it a special durability and resistance to attack by termites. It was for these reasons that it was sought after in India in ancient times for temple construction. More recently, it was used extensively for railway sleepers and as construction timber for beams, flooring, posts, door and window frames, furniture and carved sacred icons, as well as for bridges, vehicle bodies, masts and spars.

The cedar of Lebanon, meanwhile, was also widely utilized over a large geographical area. It was used by the Mesopotamians, whose civilization flourished some 4,000 years before the birth of Christ; by the ancient kings of Assyria (from about 2500 BC); and by the rulers of neighbouring countries, especially for building and embellishing their palaces. Egyptian builders are said to have imported the wood before 3000 BC – some of it for carving figures and for making sarcophagi. The oily nature of the wood meant that it was preferred to other woods because it deterred attack by insects (and perhaps stopped them from disturbing the dead). Famous sea-faring peoples, including the Phoenicians and Venetians, were also to make extensive use of cedar wood for their navies.

But perhaps the most famous use of cedar of Lebanon wood was for the construction of King Solomon's temple in Jerusalem. The third king of Israel, King Solomon (*c*.1015–977 BC) built his temple and royal palaces on a magnificent scale. Other great buildings, as well as 'a chariot of the wood of Lebanon' (Song of Solomon 3:9) were also constructed for this great king. The Bible records that Solomon sent a letter to King Hiram of Tyre (today known as Soûr, a port in south-west Lebanon) requesting him to: 'Do business with me as you did with my father, King David, when you sold him cedar logs for building his palace. I am building a temple to honour the Lord my God …' (2 Chronicles 2:3–4).

In order to do this, Solomon sent over 180,000 men to cut down the trees and prepare the timber, to carry the provisions necessary, and to oversee the work. In addition, King Hiram supplied thousands of his own men to help in the felling of the trees. It was to take seven years of arduous work to complete the temple and 13 more to build Solomon's private house. King Solomon also built the 'house of the Forest of Lebanon', the great Porch of Judgement, and a house for his favourite wife – largely of cedar wood. Descriptions of the size of the temple alone,

which was 27m (88½ft) long and 9m (29½ft) wide, and had an entrance room that was 54m (177ft) high, give a good idea of the enormous quantities of cedar wood that must have been involved: 'The walls, the floor and the ceiling were built of cedar boards, and the inside walls were covered with panels of cedar … the cedar panels were decorated with carvings of gourds and flowers; the whole interior was covered with cedar, so that no stone could be seen' (I Kings 6:15–18).

It is evident that vast forests of Lebanon cedars once existed, and it is known that they formerly extended in a continuous belt from southern Lebanon to the Taurus Mountains of Turkey. However, the continuous onslaught against them for their timber, over several thousand years, has left them drastically reduced.

The regeneration of cedar forests in Lebanon has been hampered by the grazing of goats and the development of ski resorts.

Ancient survivors

The world's largest and most intact *Cedrus libani* forest is located in the Taurus Mountains of south-east Turkey. The forest covers nearly 90,000 ha. (347 sq. miles) and is part of what is considered to be the Mediterranean's most diverse ecosystem, including around 950 flowering plant species, and remote habitats for some of Eurasia's most endangered animals, such as the brown bear (*Ursus arctos*), grey wolf (*Canis lupus*), lynx (*Lynx lynx*) and caracal (*Caracal caracal*), as well as the critically endangered Anatolian leopard (*Panthera pardus* subsp. *tulliana*). In Lebanon, several cedar reserves have been created, but only remnants of the ancient forests remain. These reserves are situated in a few valleys of the Lebanon

Mountain range, by far the largest being the Shouf Cedar Nature Reserve in the mountains south-east of Beirut, which holds one quarter of Lebanon's cedars and where a project to plant 100,000 seedlings has been underway for several years. The most famous grove of ancient cedars, comprising only about 400 trees and known as the Cedars of God, is situated at about 1,890m (6,200ft), near Bcharré on the slopes of the Mount Lebanon range. The youngest big tree in this grove is said to be about 200 years old, while estimates range from 1,000 to 3,000 years for the dozen or so oldest individuals. Other small cedar forests are also to be found at Tannourine, south of Jabal Aïtou, and north of Jabal Qaraqif.

The sad decline of Lebanon's cedars has been a source of great concern to many. Exacerbating the problem over long periods of time were goats, which by browsing on cedar seedlings prevented any useful regeneration of the trees. In 1876, Queen Victoria (1819–1901) was so moved by the cedars' plight that she paid for a wall to be erected around the Cedars of God grove, in order to protect it from goats. Measures were also taken more recently to keep out grazing animals, and it is reported that stands of cedars have now begun to regenerate slowly. A much more recent threat, from a more unexpected quarter, has come from the activity of skiers, whose presence near the town of Bcharré has similarly been damaging the regenerating trees. Cedars are not difficult to grow from seed, however, and there are a large number of nurseries in Lebanon producing cedar seedlings for reforestation. Extensive replanting has also been taking place in Turkey in recent times. Unfortunately, there is some fear that global climate change could affect the growth of young cedars – through a lack of snow and a possible increase in diseases and insect infections caused by higher temperatures.

Though also extensively used in the past, and still an important timber tree in India, the deodar has fared better than the cedar of Lebanon in terms of survival, and large areas of natural forest still exist. Although deodars are often found growing amid a mixture of other trees, both broad-leaved and coniferous, they are gregarious in habit and often form pure forests. In some regions, however, such as Kashmir, organized smuggling operations have been decimating deodar forests. In the Khag-Tangmarg area, local village forest committees have been forced to defend their forests from brutal armed timber smugglers by keeping vigil throughout the night.

In Pakistan and the Indian states of Kashmir and Himachal Pradesh, a spectacular but now endangered bird, the western tragopan (a short-tailed pheasant), has been found to live only in the upper reaches of the deodar forests. With its eye-catching plumage (the male's brilliant red neck, wattle and eye patches contrasting with its reddish-brown and black feathers, which are speckled with white), this beautiful bird – itself an object of reverence – is a fitting guardian of these 'trees of the gods'.

GINKGO
The dinosaur tree

BOTANICAL NAME

Ginkgo biloba

DISTRIBUTION

Some trees surviving in the wild in the mountains of south-western China; now widely cultivated throughout the world as an ornamental.

OLDEST KNOWN LIVING SPECIMEN

Li Jiawan Grand Ginkgo King, near Guiyang, the capital of Guizhou province, China, is around 3,000 years old. It measures about 15.6m (51ft) in girth at breast height.

RELIGIOUS SIGNIFICANCE

Revered by Buddhists in China and Korea, and by followers of Shinto in Japan, the ginkgo was planted as a temple tree in antiquity.

CONSERVATION STATUS

Classified on the IUCN Red List of Threatened Species in 2011 as 'endangered'.

An ancient ginkgo tree is a spectacular sight in autumn. The tallest individuals can reach heights of over 60m (200ft), and in autumn their leaves turn from apple green to a brilliant golden yellow. Against a deep blue Asian sky, this is an awe-inspiring sight, and it is not difficult to understand why the tree was revered by Buddhists in antiquity.

The ginkgo is not only a strikingly beautiful tree, but also unlike any other tree on Earth. It falls into neither of the two main categories of trees – conifer and broad-leaved – but belongs to its very own order (Ginkgoales), of which it is now the only surviving member. The ginkgo is believed by many scientists to have been the very first tree to evolve, as it has just as many similarities with ferns as it does with trees. Western botanists often call it the maidenhair tree because of the striking resemblance of its leaves to those of the maidenhair fern.

The tree has been given various other names, however. In ancient Chinese it was called *I-cho* (duck's foot tree) since the shape of its leaves is reminiscent of a duck's webbed foot. It was also known by the Chinese as the godfather–godson tree, because a tree planted by one generation would begin to produce fruit one or two generations later. However, its most popular name, ginkgo, is the Japanese version of the Chinese ideogram which is pronounced *yin-kuo*, meaning 'silver fruit'.

The ginkgo (*Ginkgo biloba*) is a deciduous tree with a graceful grey trunk, which becomes deeply fissured with age. The tree's small leaves soften its shape, without disguising the elegant branches that rise stiffly from the main trunk. Its leaves are fan-shaped and generally have a small cleft in between the two lobes. The ginkgo is so ancient that its system of leaf veins pre-dates those found in any other living tree.

Another unique feature of the ginkgos – which like most primitive plants can be either male or female – is their method of reproduction. In 1896, as he looked down his microscope at the female ginkgo tree's ovule, the Japanese botanist Sakugoro Hirase observed for the first time the presence of a motile sperm swimming towards the waiting egg cells. From a scientific point of view, this was a remarkable discovery because motile sperm was considered to be a trait associated with evolutionarily primitive non-seed plants such as mosses and ferns. Ginkgos are clearly seed-producing trees, but here was a feature that linked it more closely to ancient non-seed plants than to the conifers and broad-leaved trees that populate the planet today.

Ginkgo leaves are highly distinctive: their system of leaf veins pre-dates those found in any other tree species.

The order to which the ginkgo belongs – Ginkgoales – can be traced back to the Permian era, almost 250 million years ago, while the genus *Ginkgo* first appears in the fossil record some 170 million years ago. To date, at least four different species of ginkgo are known to have shared the planet with the dinosaurs, making the tree a true living fossil. It has survived virtually unmodified for the last 150 million years, and it is possible that it was the very first tree to rise from the prehistoric landscape and tower over tree ferns and cycads, the ancient palm-like plants that are native to tropical and subtropical regions. Fossil records show that it was once widespread throughout the world, from China to California and from southern Europe to the island of Spitsbergen in the Arctic Circle; 30 million years ago it still formed extensive stands in the London basin.

In evolutionary terms, the ginkgo has been able to survive the many great changes that have occurred over millions of years – including the attentions of herbivorous dinosaurs and a myriad of other plant-eating organisms that evolved and later became extinct – until relatively recently. The ginkgos that once covered vast areas of the Earth for millions of years have gradually been overtaken by other competing types of tree and by the time the first humans arrived in Asia about 500,000 years ago, its range had shrunk to the Chekiang region of easternmost China and Sichuan in the far west.

GINKGO

Ginkgos extinct in the wild?

At the beginning of the twentieth century, and following other plant hunters who
had begun to descend upon countries in Asia, Ernest H. 'Chinese' Wilson, as he
became known, was lured to China by stories of extraordinary plants, such as
1,000-year-old ginkgo trees that were 30.5m (100ft) tall and had girths of 15.25m
(50ft). He made two expeditions to China, in 1907 and 1911, amassing 65,000
botanical specimens for Harvard's arboretum. In 1930, not long before his death,
Wilson declared that: '[Ginkgo] no longer exists [in Asia] in a wild state, and there
is no authentic record of its ever having been seen growing spontaneously … In
Japan, Korea, southern Manchuria, and in China proper it is known as a planted
tree only, and usually in association with religious buildings, palaces, tombs, and
old historic or geomantic sites.'

For many years it was thought that
ginkgos had become extinct in the
wild and were only to be found in
temple gardens. In the last decade,
wild ginkgo trees have been located
in remote parts of south-west China.

In 1989, nearly 60 years after Wilson's last expedition, three researchers – Peter Del Tredici from Harvard, Yang Guang, director of Nanjing Botanical Garden, and Ling Hsieh, a Chinese forester – began looking for wild ginkgos on Tian Mu Mountain in China. As they carried out their search in a forest containing a number of large ginkgo trees, it soon became apparent that there were few, if any, young trees. However, what the three did notice was that many of the large old trees were reproducing vigorously from suckers. Aerial roots known as chichi had been observed in ginkgo trees before, but on Tian Mu Mountain they witnessed lignotubers emerging from the base of trees for the first time. Their presence helps to explain how ginkgos can live so for so long, outliving pests and diseases and sending out new sprouts when damaged or stressed.

Recent DNA analyses also support the theory that there are indeed wild populations still surviving in China. Research has shown that isolated ginkgo populations in south-western China, especially around the southern slopes of Jinfo Mountain, have a significantly higher degree of genetic diversity than populations in other parts of the country. It is believed that south-western China may have provided a glacial refuge for ginkgo populations in the wild.

OPPOSITE
A giant ginkgo tree in South Korea that is believed to be more than 1,000 years old.

BELOW
Trees such as the giant ginkgo at Yon Mun temple in South Korea attract thousands of visitors each year.

Ancient individuals

The largest *Ginkgo biloba* in the world, the Li Jiawan Grand Ginkgo King, is located about 100 km (62 miles) west of Guiyang, the capital of Guizhou province in China. It stands about 30m (98ft) tall, with a girth of 15.6m (51ft) at breast height. At its widest, the trunk is 5.8m (19ft) wide. The trunk is largely hollow, enclosing an area of around 10–12 sq. m (108–130 sq. ft), which is said to be large enough to seat a dinner party of ten!

Chinese researchers have described this giant as a 'five-generations-in-one-tree' complex. Such trees occur when a seedling takes root as a tree and then over the course of hundreds, possibly thousands of years – as a result of repeated sprouting in places where a trunk has been damaged or died – a new trunk forms and continues the tree's growth and development. In the case of the Ginkgo King there are five distinct, partly fused trunks visible. Researchers believe that first-generation trunks may reach up to 1,200 years of age, that second generation stems live for about 1,000 years, and that subsequent trunks decrease in age by 200 years per generation. Using this formula, the maximum age for the Ginkgo King would be around 4,000 to 4,500 years old.

There are a number of other large ginkgos in China, including the Ginkgo Queen, which is reputed to be 2,500 years old. A tree in Lengji, Luding Xian, in the province of Sichuan, is 30m (98ft) tall and has a girth of 12.4m (40½ft) at breast height. It is said to have been planted when Zhu Geliang went on an expedition to southern Sichuan during the period known as the Three Kingdoms, which would make it more than 1,700 years old. Another specimen in Lijiawan, Guizhou province in China is 40m (131ft) tall and has a diameter of 4.71m (15¾ft).

Set in a dramatic mountain landscape, the tallest ginkgo today stands in the grounds of the much-visited Yon Mun temple in South Korea, about 96 km (60 miles) north of Seoul. It is a magnificent and very healthy tree, over 60m (200ft) tall, and displays the ginkgo's classic conical shape. The trunk is 4.5m (15ft) thick at breast height and the tree is reputed to be 1,100 years old.

Another of the largest ginkgo trees in South Korea measures 13m (42½ft) around the trunk, and is estimated to be at least 800 years old. Local legend records that the tree grew from a stick dropped by a Buddhist priest who stopped to drink the water from a stream. Local people revere this tree, as legend has it that a huge white snake lives inside. Some also believe that there will be a bumper harvest if the tree's leaves all turn yellow at once. Some large trees also occur in Japan, in Shinto temple grounds, although it is believed that these trees were introduced less than 1,000 years ago. The magnificent Tenjinsama no ichou, for example, which is to be found in Aomori, North Honshu, Japan, has a girth of around 10m (33ft) and is spectacularly festooned with chichi or aerial roots. Today 11.5 per cent of Japan's street trees are ginkgos. They make ideal urban trees because they are resistant to pollution and disease, and at 100 years old are still flourishing when many other street trees have long since died of old age or disease.

OPPOSITE
The distinctive shape of the ginkgo leaf has given rise to one of the tree's popular Chinese names – 'duck's foot tree'.

The German naturalist and physician Engelbert Kaempfer provided the Western world with its first description of the ginkgo at the end of the seventeenth century. Ginkgos were then introduced from Japan to Europe in about 1730. Large trees of over 200 years of age can be seen in Britain – the oldest is at the Royal Botanic Gardens, Kew, just outside London, having been transferred there in 1761 from the Duke of Argyll's estate not far away in Twickenham. After an absence of 30 million years, the ginkgo is once more thriving in the London basin.

Ginkgo biloba is very hardy and will thrive in a wide range of conditions. It is able to tolerate the polluted air of major cities and is highly resistant to pests and diseases. Horticulturalists have been quick to exploit the natural variations that exist, in order to select and breed many ornamental forms. In autumn, the falling fruit of the female tree tends to make the area beneath the tree malodorous, so it is male trees that are generally planted as ornamentals in large cities.

The demand for ginkgos

The ginkgo's leaves and seeds have a very long history of use in traditional Chinese medicine for the treatment of a variety of ailments, including asthma and lung complaints. Stewed ginkgo seeds (the seeds are toxic when raw) are prescribed by modern Chinese practitioners as a general lung tonic and for the treatment of asthma and bronchitis.

While the seeds feature most prominently in the ancient Chinese materia medica, it is the active compounds contained within the leaves that have given rise to ginkgo's fame in more recent times as a possible treatment for several medical conditions. Ginkgo extracts are now worth millions of dollars annually, and, in the form of supplements, are among the best-selling herbal medicines in Europe. Much recent research has been prompted by the discovery that ginkgo improves blood circulation by dilating blood vessels and reducing the stickiness of blood platelets, and can therefore improve the flow of blood to the brain. As a result, ginkgo has been widely prescribed in Europe for a whole range of ailments that might benefit from increased blood flow, from senile dementia, tinnitus and memory loss to chilblains and Raynaud's disease. Opinion is divided, however, as to the real benefit of ginkgo in this regard. While some studies have shown that ginkgo may have a positive effect on memory in people with Alzheimer's disease, several studies have found that ginkgo was no better than a placebo in reducing the symptoms of Alzheimer's or actually preventing it, and no better than a placebo in relieving tinnitus.

To meet the world demand for ginkgo products for the pharmaceutical industry, China has promoted the cultivation of ginkgos by farmers. Millions of trees are also being raised on plantations in the United States, France, South Korea and Japan for the export of their leaves to Europe.

Ginkgo fruit

The pinkish-yellow fruits that develop are small, plum-like and hang in pairs. They are, however, notorious for their unpleasant smell. Harvard ginkgo expert Peter Del Tredici was curious about why the fruits smelled so bad. However, once he learned that nocturnal hunters such as Chinese leopard cats and masked palm civets, attracted by the smell of rotting flesh, ate the fruits, he postulated that the seeds needed to pass through the gut of animals to aid germination. His experiments revealed that after passing through the gut, germination rates increased from 15–71 per cent. Ginkgos have existed for so long that it is interesting to speculate on the kind of primitive mammals or dinosaurs that might have eaten these fruit 150 million years ago.

Despite the toxic outer coating of the ginkgo fruit, the seeds inside have long been prized as a food. The whitish or silvery nuts are cracked open to reveal the kernel, which – after roasting – is eaten as a delicacy in the Far East.

Koreans collect the fruits for both food and medicine. Roasted ginkgo kernels are sold on the streets of large cities such as Seoul, while the fruits are used to make remedies for coughs, bladder complaints and asthma. In modern China, alongside their medicinal uses, the fruit are still served at wedding feasts as a symbol of fertility. Other uses include a detergent for washing clothes and a cosmetics ingredient.

Temple gardens
The saviours of the ginkgo are the religious orders – Buddhists in China and Korea, and followers of Shinto in Japan – who cultivated them in early times. Today, the very finest examples of the ginkgo are to be found growing in temple gardens in these three countries. It is not clear exactly why ginkgos were adopted as temple trees, but their re-emergence as ornamentals was noted as far back as the eighth century.

Bibliography

Arburrow, Y., *The Enchanted Forest* (Capall Bann Publishing, 1993)

Bean, W. J. and eds, *Trees and Shrubs Hardy in the British Isles* (John Murray, 8th edition revised, 1970)

Best, E., '*The Maori Canoe*' (Dominion Museum Bulletin, no. 7, 1925; reprinted by the Government Printer, Wellington, 1976)

Bierhorst, J., *Mitos Y Leyendas do Los Aztecas* (Editorial Edaf, 1984)

Bosely, D., Jensen, J. and Sinclair, M., *California* (Rough Guides, 1996)

Boyer, M. F., *Tree Talk* (Thames & Hudson, 1996) Bradt, H., *Guide to Madagascar* (Bradt Publications, UK, 1997)

Bradt, H., Schuurman, D. and Garbutt, N., *Madagascar Wildlife* (Bradt Publications, UK, 1996)

Brown, M., *Dorset: Customs, Curiosities & Country Lores* (Ensign Publications, 1990)

Carder, A., *Forest Giants of the World Past and Present* (Fitzhenry & Whiteside, 1995)

Cavalcante, P. B., *Frutas Comestíiveis da Amazônia* (Edições Cejup, 1991)

Chetan, A. and Brueton, D., *The Sacred Yew* (Arkana Penguin Books, 1994)

Collins, M. (ed.), *The Last Rainforests* (Mitchell Beazley, 1995)

Dockrill, A.W., *Australian Indigenous Orchids* (Surrey Beatty & Sons, 1992)

Edlin, H. L. and Nimmo, M. et al., *The Illustrated Encyclopedia of Trees* (Salamander Books, 1978)

Ell, G., *King Kauri* (Bush Press, New Zealand, 1996)

Ell, G., *Kauri, Past and Present* (Bush Press, 1994)

Elliot, W. R. and Jones, D. L., *Encyclopaedia of Australian Plants*, vol. 7 (Lothian Books, 1997)

Elsasser, A. B., *Indians of Sequoia and King's Canyon National Parks* (Sequoia Natural History Association, 1962)

Else, D., Murray, J. and Swaney D., *Africa: The South* (Lonely Planet, 1997)

Enright, N.J. and Hill, R. S., *Ecology of the Southern Conifers* (Melbourne University Press, 1995)

Escobar, B., Matthews, K. and White, D., '*Pieces of the Puzzle*', in *The Garden* (December 1998)

Evelyn, J., *Sylva* (Stobart & Son, facsimile edition, 1979)

Farjon, A., *A Natural History of Conifers* (Timber Press Inc., 2008)

Fichtner, C, *Gesegnete Brunnen* (Landsberger Verlagsanstalt, 1992)

Floyd, A. G., *Rainforest Trees of Mainland South-eastern Australia* (Inkata Press, 1989)

Fröhlich, H.J., *Alte Liebenswerte Bäume in Deutschland* (Cornelia Ahlering Verlag, 1989)

Gentry A. H., *Woody Plants of Northwest South America* (Conservation International, 1996)

Goerss, H., *Unsere Baumveteranen* (Landbuch Verlag, GmbH, 1981)

Grieve, H., *A Modern Herbal* (Penguin Books, 1984; first published by Jonathan Cape, 1931)

Guppy R, *Wai-Wai* (John Murray, 1958)

Hageneder, F., *Yew – A History* (Sutton Publishing, 2007)

Harden, G.J. (ed.), *Flora of New South Wales*, vol. 1 (Royal Botanic Gardens, Sydney, 1990)

Hart, C., *British Trees in Colour* (Michael Joseph, 1973)

Hayward, B.W., *Kauri Gum and the Gumdiggers* (Bush Press, Auckland, 1989)

Holliday, I., *A Field Guide to Australian Trees* (Landsdowne Publishing, 1995; first published by Rigsby Publishers, 1969)

Hora, B. (ed.), *The Oxford Encyclopedia of Trees of the World* (Oxford University Press, 1981)

Hight, J., *Britain's Tree Story: The History and Legends of Britain's Ancient Trees.* (National Trust Books, 2011)

Huxley, F, *Affable Savages* (Hart-Davis, 1956)

Jiménez,V., *El Arbol de El Tule En La Historia* (Codex Editores, 1990)

Johnson, H., Encyclopedia of Trees (Mitchell Beazley, 1984)

Johnson, H., *The International Book of Trees* (Mitchell Beazley, 1973)

Johnson, O., *Champion Trees of Britain and Ireland* (Kew Publishing, 2011)

Jones, W. R., *Yosemite, The Story Behind the Scenery* (KC Publications, 1989)

Jones, W. G., Hill, K. D. and Allen, J. M., '*Wollemia nobilis, a new living Australian genus and species in the Araucariaceae*', in Telopea, vol. 6 (2–3), (March-September 1995)

Jordan, M., *Plants of Mystery and Magic* (Blandford, 1997)

Keen, L., *Guide to Lebanon* (Bradt Publications, UK, 1995)

Kelley, M. S., *Congress Trail: Sequoia National Park* (Sequoia Natural History Association, 1978)

Lewington, A., *Plants for People* (Natural History Museum, 1990)

Lewington, A., *Plants for People* (Eden Project Books, 2003)

Mabberley D. J., *The Plant-Book* (Cambridge University Press, 1989)

McCrea, B., Pinchuck,T and Mthembu-Salter, G., *South Africa, Lesotho & Swaziland* (Rough Guides, 1997)

McIntyre, C, *Namibia*, (Bradt Publications, UK, 1998)

McLaughlan, G., *Insight Guides: New Zealand* (APA Publications (HK), 1995) Maiden, J. H. *The Forest Flora of New South Wales*, vol. VII (John Spence, Acting Government Printer, 1922)

Manchao, C, *The Origin of Chinese Deities* (Foreign Languages Press, Beijing, 1997)

Margolin, M. (ed.), *The Way We Lived: Californian Indian Stories, Songs and Reminiscences* (Heyday Books, 1993; first published 1991)

Marren, P., *Woodland Heritage* (David & Charles, 1990)

Matus, M., *Los Zapotecas Binni Záa* (Dirección General de Culturas Populares, 1991),

Menninger, E. A., *Fantastic Trees* (Timber Press, 1995)

Milner, J. E., *The Tree Book* (Collins & Brown, 1992)

Milton, J., *Paradise Lost* (ed. Fowler, A.), (Longman, 1971)

Mitchell, A., *Alan Mitchell's Trees of Britain* (HarperCollins, 1996)

Mitchell, A., *A Field Guide to the Trees of Britain and Northern Europe* (William Collins, reprinted 1986)

Moldenke, H. N. and A.L., *Plants of the Bible* (Dover Publications, 1986)

Nairn, B., Serle, G. and Ward, R. (section eds), *Australian Dictionary of Biography*, vol. 5 (Melbourne University Press, n.d.)

North, M., 'In Pursuit of the Puzzle-Monkeys in Chili', in *Pall Mall Gazette* (11 March 1885)

Oldfield, S., Lusty, C. and MacKinven, A. (eds), *The World List of Threatened Trees* (World Conservation Press, 1998)

Opie, I., *Dictionary of Superstition* (Oxford, 1989)

Packenham, T. *The Remarkable Baobab* (Weidenfeld & Nicholson, 2004)

Pakenham,T, *Meetings with Remarkable Trees* (Weidenfeld & Nicolson, 1996) Parmer, E. and Pitman N., *Trees of South Africa* (A. A. Balkema, 1961)

Paterson, J. M., *Tree Wisdom* (Thorsons, 1996)

Pickering, D., *Dictionary of Superstition* (Cassell, 1985)

Porteous, A., *The Lore of the Forest* (Senate, 1996; first published by Allen & Unwin, 1928)

Rackham, O., *Trees and Woodland in the British Landscape* (J. M. Dent, 1976) Radford, E. and M.A., *Encylopedia of Superstition* (Hutchinson, 1969)

Riley, M., *New Zealand Trees & Ferns* (Viking Sevenseas, 1983)

Rosenblum, M., Olives, *The Life and Lore of a Noble Fruit* (Absolute Press, 1996)

Sahni, K. C, *The Book of Indian Trees* (Bombay Natural History Society/Oxford University Press, 1998)

Salmon, J.T., *The Reed Field Guide to New Zealand Native Trees* (Reed Books, 1996; first published 1986)

Sastri, B. N. (chief ed.), *The Wealth of India* (Delhi, 1950)

Silcock, L. (ed.), *The Rainforests, A Celebration* (Barrie & Jenkins, 1989)

Sisitka, L. et al., *Guide to the Care of Ancient Trees* (English Nature, 1996)

Smart, R., *Trees and Woodlands of Cheshire* (Cheshire Landscape Trust, 1992)

Stokes, J and R. D., *The Heritage Trees of Britain and Northern Ireland* (Constable, 2004)

Venter, F. and J. A., *Making the Most of Indigenous Trees* (Briza Publications, 1996)

Vickery R., *Oxford Dictionary of Plant Lore* (Oxford University Press, 1995) Wallace, A. R., *A Narrative of Travels on the Amazon and Rio Negro* (Ward, Lock, 1889)

Werner, E.T. C, *Myths & Legends of China* (Graham Brash, Singapore, 1984; reprinted 1995)

White, E., *The Flowering of Gondwana* (Princeton University Press, 1990)

White, J., *Estimating the Age of Large and Veteran Trees in Britain* (Information Note: Forestry Commission, November 1998)

Wildwood, C, *The Encyclopedia of Healing Plants* (Piatkus, 1997)

Williamson, R., *The Great Yew Forest* (Macmillan, 1978)

Wilson, E.H., *China: Mother of Gardens* (Benjamin Blom Inc, 1971)

Woodcock, M. W, 'The Auracaria Imbricata or Monkey Puzzle Tree', in *The Tree Lover*, vol. 3 (1941)

Woodward, M. (ed.), *Gerard's Herball* (Bracken Books, 1985)

A number of issues of the following journals were also consulted:

Economic Botany (New York Botanic Garden); *Kew* (Royal Botanic Gardens, Kew); *New Scientist* (Reed Business Information Ltd); *Non-Wood Forest Products* (FAO, Rome) Non-Wood News (FAO, Rome); *Plant Talk* (National Tropical Botanic Garden); *Tree News*, (Think Publishing); *Yew News* (Conservation Foundation)

The following websites may also be useful :

General
www.conifers.org
www.panda.org
www.kew.org
www.monumentaltrees.com
www.wikipedia.org
www.europeanancienttrees.com/
www.sanasi.org

www.globaltrees.org
www.cathedralgrove.eu

UK
www.ancienttreehunt.org.uk
www.treeregister.org
www.woodland-trust.org.uk/ancient-tree-forum
www.woodlandtrust.org.uk
www.nationaltrust.org.uk
www.kew.org/plants-fungi/
www.ancient-yew.org

USA
www.savetheredwoods.org
www.nps.gov/seki/
www.nps.gov/grba/planyourvisit/identifying-
bristlecone-pines.htm

Mexico
www.conifers.org/cu/Taxodium_mucronatum.php
www.treesofnorthamerica.net/trees/
Taxodium+Mucronatum

Chile
www.globaltrees.org/ps_mp_chile.htm

New Zealand
www.notabletrees.org.nz
www.doc.govt.nz/conservation/native-plants/kauri
www.terranature.org/kauri.htm
www.communities.co.nz/WaipouaForest
www.teara.govt.nz/en/conifers/4/3
www.conifers.org/po/Podocarpus_totara.php

Australia
www.rbgsyd.nsw.gov.au

South Africa/Madagascar
www.scientific-web.com/en/Biology/Plants/
Magnoliophyta/Adansonia.html
www.dendro.co.za/uploads/2/8/2/1/2821110/nrbtsa.pdf

Spain
http://www.bosquessinfronteras.org/
http://trepalari.org/paginas_interes.htm
http://www.aearboricultura.org/

Belgium
http://www.duizendjarigeeik.be/
http://www.monumentaltrees.com/en/

Hungary
http://dendromania.hu/index.php?old=linkek

Germany
http://www.championtrees.de/

Netherlands
http://www.boombastik.nl/
http://www.bomenstichting.nl/

Poland
http://www.deby.bialowieza.pl/index.php5

Switzerland
http://www.proarbore.com/startseite

Greece
www.europeanancienttrees.com/greece.html

Lebanon
www.conifers.org/pi/Cedrus_libani.php

Acknowledgements

Many people helped us to undertake the research and photography both for this new edition and the first edition (in the late 1990s) of *Ancient Trees*, and we are greatly indebted to them all.

For their assistance with this new edition we would particularly like to thank Tony Kirkham (Royal Botanic Gardens, Kew), Ted Green (Ancient Tree Forum), Professor Donald Piggott, Fred Hageneder (Ancient Yew Group), and Jeroen Philippona (Monumentaltrees.com).

We would also like to thank the personnel of the Ancient Tree Forum, including Jill Butler, Neville Fay, Brian Muelaner, Caroline Davis, John Smith, David Clayden and William Cathcart, who are working hard to protect our ancient tree heritage both here in the UK and across the world.

Assistance from the Ancient Yew Group was also very much appreciated, and we would like to thank Tim Hills in particular.

Edward Parker would like to thank all those who collaborated or worked with him on the Ancient Tree Hunt (2009–2011) at The Woodland Trust, including Katherine Owen, David Alderman, Nikki Williams, Louise Hackett, James Storey, Alison Evershed, Jill Butler, Jon Parsons, Fiona Moss, Chris Hickman, Ann Rooney, Mark Brown, Tanya Burton, Michelle Davis, Sharon Wennekers, Rhiannon Bates and the many other staff at the Woodland Trust who supported and encouraged the work on ancient trees. He would also like to thank Rob McBride, Steve Waters, Tony Burgoyne, Howard Leader, Vanessa Champion and all the other ATH volunteer verifiers whose hard work and time spent finding, recording and verifying the UK's ancient trees was a constant inspiration.

Anna Lewington would particularly like to thank John Short for his advice and invaluable help with the Index to this new edition.

For the first edition of *Ancient Trees*, we are particularly indebted to Francis Sullivan and Alison Lucas, formerly of the World Wide Fund for Nature (WWF) UK, who not only provided funding for the initial research trips to Australia and New Zealand, but had faith in the project from the start.

Many other people assisted or were consulted during the research and writing of the original book, including the following members, or former members, of staff at the Royal Botanic Gardens, Kew: Dr Aljos Farjon, Dr Pat Griggs, Dr Stuart Henchie, Tony Kirkham, Dr Geoffrey Kite, Barbara Lowry, Anne Marshall, Laura Ponsonby, Helen Sanderson and Dr Jeffrey Wood. Members or former members of WWF in different parts of the world also assisted, including Sandra Charity, Dr Chris Elliott, Dr Alan Hamilton, Dr Steve Howard, Dr Lei Guangchun, Peter Newborn and Michael Rae.

Expert advice and statistical information was also kindly provided for the first edition by David Alderman (Director), Pamela Stevenson (Secretary & Treasurer) and John White, (Technical Adviser) of the Tree Register of the British Isles.

Other organizations that gave assistance include: Royal Society for the Protection of Birds; World Pheasant Association; Goethe Institute; German National Tourist Office; Comite Nacional pro Defensa de la Fauna y Flora (Codeff), Chile.

Individuals we thank again (listed with the posts they held at the time) include: Ian Aldred (Cheshire County Council); Mark Atterton (World Conservation Monitoring Centre); Brian Ayres (Archaeology and Environment Department, Norfolk County Council); Laura Battlebury (World Conservation Monitoring Centre); Dr Jeffrey Chambers (University of California, Santa Barbara); Patrick Curry (Friends of the Ankerwyke Yew); Dr Martin Gardner (Edinburgh Botanic Garden); John Gittens (Cheshire Landscape Trust); Anna Hallett (Royal Botanic Gardens, Sydney); Dr Sawsan Khuri (University of Reading); Dr Antonio Lara (Universidad Austral, Chile); Herr Hannich (Schenklengsfeld Town Council); Niro Higuchi (Instituto Nacional de Pesquisas da Amazonia, Manaus); Garth Nikles (Queensland Forest Research Institute); Nick Lawrence (Dorchester Reference Library); Jeroen Pater ('Monumental Trees' project); Libby Simon (Conservation Foundation); Dr Tim Synott (Forest Stewardship Council, Oaxaca); Rachel Thackray (Thackray Forrester Communications); Sonia Williams (Crawley Library).

Thanks are also due to the following individuals: Anand Chetan, John Gilchrist, Jack Weber, Richard Dodge, Reynaldo and Alfredo Melihir, Reynaldo Mariqueo,Stephen King, Richard Head, Ray Oddi, Wilma Rittershausen, Lucinda Lachlin. The work of Canadian botanist Al Carder was also a great inspiration.

We are very grateful to friends and family for their support and encouragement while we updated the original book, and in particular: Peter, Edwina, Richard, Charles and Emma Parker, Sherry Tolputt, Jay Griffiths, Hannah Scrase, Scott Poynton, Kath Owen, Bryan and Cherry Alexander, Sarah Oldridge and Archie Miles.

Finally, we must thank Tina Persaud, and our patient editor Nicola Newman, both of Anova Books, as well as Gina Fullerlove of the Royal Botanic Gardens, Kew, who made this new edition of *Ancient Tree*s a reality.

While acknowledging the help that so many individuals and organizations have given us, we must also point out that any mistakes or errors remain entirely our own.

Picture credits

Index

Anna Lewington is a well-known ethnobotanist and writer. Her previous books include *Plants for People* and several educational books for children. She took part in the first series of BBC TV's 'Rough Science'.

Edward Parker is a renowned and prize-winning photographer and writer who specializes in environmental issues, travel and education. He has worked in more than 30 countries, and most recently was the project manager of the Woodland Trust's Ancient Tree Hunt.

To receive regular email updates on forthcoming Anova titles, email update@anovabooks.com with your area of interest in the subject field.

Visit www.anovabooks.com for a full list of our available titles.